is an interpretive study of Shake-
... which does not concern
... blems,

THE SHATTERED GLASS:

A Dramatic Pattern
in Shakespeare's Early Plays

THE
SHATTERED
GLASS:

A Dramatic Pattern
in Shakespeare's
Early Plays

by John P. Cutts
Wayne State University

Wayne State University Press, Detroit
1968

Contents

5

Preface

the substance of [*his*] *first act*
Will be shadows, and the strife with shadows
. . . .
Shall he who held the solid substance
Wander waking with deceitful shadows?

Textual Note

All quotations and line numberings are taken from the following text: W. A. Neilson and C. J. Hill (eds.), *The Complete Plays and Poems of William Shakespeare* (Cambridge, Mass., 1942).

Introduction

Many and various have been the explanations given for Shakespeare's finding himself as a dramatist exploiting one by one the possibilities of prevailing patterns in comedy, history-chronicle, and tragedy, from Roman comedy and commedia dell'arte to Lylyan comedy of highly sophisticated language, from chronicle-history to chronic historical (and sometimes hysterical) disaster consequent on the disruption of a right sense of order, from Marlovian heroes of the absolute almost diabolically possessed with one ambition pursued with all Senecan trappings, to a hero mesmerized by the shadow he casts. All approaches, provided they are not restrictive and exclusive of one another, tend to furnish a valuable framework within which we can go on asking relevant questions and suggesting further methods of approach.

It was while I was engaged on a study of *Richard II,* trying to account for the play's emergence from a chronicle-history into a remarkable piece of stagecraft, that I detected a pattern which seemed to reveal one of Shakespeare's techniques of dramatic highlighting. When Richard shatters the glass he has looked into through his misty veil of tears the play, too, shatters into a new and more powerful dramatic life. The shattered glass is obviously a fitting climax to the emotion-packed imagery of Richard's self-imposed out-Christing stance, of the well-buckets and the snow king, but, unlike them, it offers possibilities of being used by the dramatist time and again without the risk of palling through patent repetition.

It is as if the play had suddenly found not only a remarkable point of focus from which it could itself be more interestingly viewed, but also as if the play had opened up for Shakespeare exceptional ways of his being powerfully dramatic in future writings. The shattered glass breaks the "brittle glass" (*Richard III* IV.ii.62) of earlier dramatic experimentations. Man himself must not only shatter but also be shattered, must be broken down into the many people within one person, none of them contented, and made as aware of this as his intellectual endowment will allow.

Shakespeare did not suddenly hit on this shattered glass pattern with *Richard II,* to be sure, but it seems possible to suggest that it was not until Richard II literally shattered that glass that Shakespeare realized how much he had been leaning toward such a dramatic show. His so-called earliest plays, and it really does not matter for present purposes what the exact order of the early plays is purported to be—critics disagree about the order but at least agree about which plays they are trying to order thus—are a foreshadowing of such a dramatic technique. This study concentrates on mirror imagery, substance and shadow, seeing and unseeing, fragmentation and synthesis, showing how Shakespeare was finding his way toward making his dramatis personae shatter their own brittleness, their own puppetry, into a new and more powerful dramatic life.

THE EARLY COMEDIES

The Comedy of Errors

The lasting interest of *The Comedy of Errors*, I suggest, lies in the inability of its dramatis personae to see beyond the mirror of identical twins, to see any further than outward semblances. Master and servant, husband and wife, tradesman and client know no more about each other than what mistakenly they *see* in a glass, nor do they realize they are seeing darkly. We may, of course, suggest that the characters are stock classical and / or commedia dell'arte representations, but whether we agree with this, there are good reasons for suggesting that the Dromios, the nearest counterparts to the classical and commedia forbears, are intrinsic to *The Comedy of Errors* not because they are *characters*, but because they make us see *double:* they make us see the problems at least twice over, and are indeed quite natural consequences of not seeing right the first time. The comedy of mistaken identity, brilliantly handled though it is with Shakespeare doubling the twins and manipulating far more skilfully than Lyly in *Mother Bombie*, is not just Shakespeare rehandling Plautine and Lylyan material and demonstrating how much better he can do the job than either of these dramatists. He is finding his way toward something that can be inimitably his own, not just in adaptation, but in the very framework and *structure* itself.

When the mistaken identities are cleared up there is

little to suggest that any of the characters considers his "seeing" was at fault, though the nearest implication is that Adriana's shrewishness blinded her. The overall impression of the play is that man is *bewitched,* that uncanny powers are awake manipulating him. That the play is brilliant in this puppetry sense is glaringly patent; what is by no means so obvious is why man allows himself to be a puppet. And here the significance of the tragic note of Aegeon is indispensable when we consider that this failure to see right is not just a laughing matter but fraught with tragic propensities both for the unseers and for those within the immediate "unseeing" focus; that man's unseeing actions have repercussions far beyond his wildest dreams and fears. With Antipholus of Syracuse we ask, "was I married to her in my dream? / Or sleep I now and think I hear all this? / What error drives our eyes and ears amiss?" (II.ii.184–86).

How comes it that man "Smoth'red in errors, feeble, shallow, weak" (III.ii.35), estranged from his "dear self's better part" (II.ii.125), "transformed" both "in mind and in . . . shape" (II.ii.199) makes such a complete ass of himself? He is apparently "Known unto [others], and to [him] self disguis'd" (II.ii.216), because he has not taken anything like a good look at himself yet, though Antipholus of Syracuse's witty rejoinder to the first merchant's commending him to his own content, "He that commends me to mine own content / Commends me to the thing I cannot get" (I.ii.33–34) has possible introspective overtones, however momentary. Man in *The Comedy of* [human] *Errors* is easily "lost," "perplexed" and "bewitched," played upon by external forces not necessarily puckish. For the most part he does not yet know whether the gods are just or no, or whether he should even know to ask the question.

14

With Antipholus of Syracuse we are sufficiently puzzled by the play's situations to ask "What error drives [men's] eyes and ears amiss?" (II.ii.186), but we are in a better position than he to estimate why he "entertain[s] the [offer'd] fallacy" (II.ii.188) in the hope of finding out more about "this sure uncertainty" (II.ii.187).

On one level it is obviously sheerly ludicrous that he should be greeted by Adriana, whom he has never in his life seen before, as husband, and chided for not giving her the assurance of the chain of fair marriage "quarter with his bed" (II.i.108). On another it is exceedingly appropriate that this marriage estrangement should reflect his own sense of loss "like a drop of water / That in the ocean seeks another drop" (I.ii.35–36). Adriana forcibly reminds him of the binding quality of the chain to her which to break is as difficult as to retrieve a "drop of water in the breaking gulf" unmingled and "[w]ithout addition or diminishing" (II.ii.128,130). Antipholus of Syracuse nominally in search of "a mother and a brother" (I.ii.39) does run the enormous risk of losing himself in the breaking gulf, of foundering his ship, Aegeon-wise, on the "mighty rock" of inquisitive unseeing (I.ii.38), because he hardly knows what he is looking for or "if that [he is he]" (III.ii.41).

His coming to Ephesus in one sense reflects his growing concern with the discontent which is himself, and in another his escape from self—his decision to "wander up and down" to weary his identity with restless motion and "in this mist at all adventures go" (II.ii.218). Not until his self is symbolically returned to him in the "glass" (V.i.417) of his image at the very end of the play is the dream texture of his existence shattered into something like reality, and he is in amity with his identity, but ironically he hardly knows how to accept it as reality since his happiness of discovery is concerned with Luciana, who would never have appeared to him if error had not driven his "eyes and ears amiss."

He literally recovers a mother, father and brother, and gains a wife as the play's comedy of errors rectifies its situational self, but the real significance is that he has found a rounded out complete family identity, and in a way that is "past thought of human reason" (V.i.189), not by "Fixing [his] eyes on whom [his] care was fix'd" (I.i.85), but by losing himself "confound[ing] himself" (I.ii.38), in the serio-comic "stories of [his] own mishaps" (I.i.121).

It is a careful ironic stroke of juxtaposition to have his father under sentence of death exclaim at the very end of the first scene "Hopeless and helpless doth Aegeon wend" and then to have Antipholus enter immediately afterward, running the very same risk as his father—"if any Syracusian born / Come to the bay of Ephesus, he dies. . . . Unless a thousand marks be levied, / To quit the penalty and to ransom him" (I.i.18–20;22–23), but with the "sure uncertainty" of his potential redemption money entrusted to a servant part of himself which he has not yet learnt to recognize, his Dromio, except to lighten his humor with his merry jests, and to be anchored at the Centaur where he can succumb to the lower part of his nature. It is only because either the presiding gods of the comedy of errors are benevolent or because stumbling man by rare accident somehow saves himself by stumbling that Antipholus's "Sleeping or waking? Mad or well-advis'd?" (II.ii.215) involvement in the banquet at Adriana's house does not transform him into the bestial victim of "Circe's cup" (V.i.270).

It is not merely coincidental that the dramatist has him describe Adriana's sister, Luciana, as a "siren" (III.ii.47) trying to drown him in her "sister's flood of tears" (III.ii.46), and call for her to "Transform [him] then" (III.ii.40)

16

by singing for herself and by unfolding the meaning of her "words' deceit" (III.ii.36) to his "earthy, gross conceit" (III.ii.34). By this means he hopes to maintain his "soul's pure truth" (III.ii.37), for she is his own "self's better part" (III.ii.61), and yet the workaday rude mechanical servant part of himself, Syracusian Dromio, who has likewise been involved with a "very beastly creature, lay[ing] claim to [him]" (III.ii.88–89) mocks his involvement by reducing it to a consideration of physical geography, centaurishly bawdy at one level—"In what part of her body stands Ireland . . . Scotland . . . France" etc. (III.ii.118,122,125,etc.) and mentally assertive at another as Dromio flees from a Circean witch who would have "transform'd [him] to a curtal dog" (III.ii.151), and "almost made [him] traitor to [him]self . . . and guilty to self-wrong" (III.ii.167–68).

What irony it is that the putative Circean banquet takes place in the Phoenix, conducive to the regenerative image of the married calm of love. Antipholus of Syracuse anchors himself temporarily at the Centaur, financially and incognitoishly secure as he thinks, and flees from recognition where he imagines "every one knows [him] and [he] know[s] none" (III.ii.157) at the Phoenix. He mistakes the Centaur for the Phoenix and the Phoenix for the Centaur. What error drives his eyes and ears amiss.

His case is both closely paralleled and carefully complemented by his Ephesian self. Antipholus of Ephesus is escaping from his identity too. This is the pointed irony of his being faced with his own rude mechanical servant self, Ephesian Dromio, who charges that he "did deny [his] wife and house" (III.i.9). The humor of the error of Ephesian Dromio mistaking Syracusian Antipholus for his master obviously carries the moment in the comedy of errors, but the underlying reflection may be much more important.

17

Ephesian Antipholus's "own handwriting would tell" (III.i.14) on the parchment of his own skin (III.i.13) what his servant sense would tell him if he knew how to recognize it. The metaphorical beating he gives this servant sense is a vain attempt to ignore its lesson.

The very first introduction of Antipholus of Ephesus in the play shows him trying to create the image of a displaced Antipholus, shut out from his house and from his marital bed by a shrewish wife. The jeweled necklace of a chain which he is commissioning at the goldsmith's, Angelo's, is ironically to afford him both an excuse for not having been at home—"Say that I linger'd with you at your shop" (III.i.3), and much more significantly a decoy of a "fair presence" (III.ii.13)—vice appareled "like virtue's harbinger" (III.ii.12), but its most serious significance lies in the fact that it is the symbol of the marriage chain he is trying to run away from and of the "unlawful love" (V.i.51) that he is running to link himself with.

But his unseduced servant self (Syracusian Dromio now within the Phoenix) belies him by asking, "Dost thou conjure for wenches, that thou calls't for such store / When one is one too many?" (III.i.34–35). It is exactly fitting that he should be literally shut out from the house and bed that he has obviously been neglecting. Adriana's fears that her husband's "company must do his minions grace, / Whilst [she] at home starve[s] for a merry look" (II.i.87–88) is hardly to be dismissed by her sister Luciana's charge that she is suffering from "Self-harming jealousy" (II.i.102), when so soon afterwards Luciana can plead with her brother-in-law to "if [he] like elsewhere, do it by stealth" (III.ii.7).

There is no doubt that Antipholus of Ephesus is attempting to escape from the chain of marriage. This is the force of his remark to Angelo for not having brought him the

18

jeweled chain—"Belike you thought our love would last too long / If it were chain'd together, and therefore came not" (IV.i.25–26), and this the powerful significance of his not having "the present money" (IV.i.34) to pay for the chain and being arrested at Angelo's suit for denying receipt of the chain. It is doubly fitting that he thinks he has sent his servant self (Syracusian Dromio) home for money to buy off the arrest, and then is faced instead with the "rope's end" of his basic servant self (Ephesian Dromio). The rope's end had been ostensibly commissioned to "bestow / Among [his] wife and [her] confederates / For locking [him] out of [his] doors by day" (IV.i.16–18), but Antipholus of Ephesus ends up beating his basic servant self.

The comedy, of course, is close to slapstick, master beating servant misunderstanding and misunderstood, but on a more solid level it points to the technique of punishing oneself at one remove, projecting one's guilt on the "obvious" target, until the "living dead" (V.i.241) pinch comes —the need to be "bound and laid in some dark room" (IV.iv.97) to "pluck out these false eyes" (IV.iv.107), not of the "Dissembling harlot" (IV.iv.104) of his wife's eyes, as he fondly imagines, but of his own, if only he could understand, for "his eye / Stray'd his affection in unlawful love" (V.i.50–51).

What irony it is that Antipholus of Syracuse has to gain his temporary freedom by "gnawing with [his] teeth [his] bonds in sunder" (V.i.249), and must attempt to gain his real freedom by appealing to the Duke on the grounds of erstwhile valiant military service when he "bestrid [him] in the wars, and took / Deep scars to save [his] life" (V.i.192–93) as if past service had anything to do with present misconduct. He is metaphorically fighting for his life as much as his father Aegeon, whom he now meets most appropriately for the first time in his life, and, of course,

19

does not know how to recognize. His non recognition makes him a metamorphosed equivalent of one who has "drunk of Circe's cup" (V.i.270) and has become "mated or stark mad" (V.i.281).

"Hopeless and helpless" (I.i.158) Aegeon, Antipholus of Ephesus and Antipholus of Syracuse all wend, but fortunately their paths converge on the Abbey where the human solution to all their difficulties is to be found in Aemilia, who has "gone in travail" (V.i.400) of her own particular variety for thirty-three years, and has not been delivered of of her identityless burden until now. Ironically Luciana accuses the Abbess of conduct ill beseeming her holiness by "separat[ing] the husband and the wife" (V.i.111), when in point of fact she herself was culpable in listening to the believed husband transferring his attention from Adriana to herself. And ironically, too, the Abbess is overhasty and unseeing in pronouncing judgment on Adriana "betray[ing] [her] to [her] own reproof" (V.i.90) of scaring her "husband from the use of wits" (V.i.86) by her "jealous fits" (V.i.85).

All of them, Aemilia, Adriana, Luciana, Aegeon, Antipholus of Syracuse, Antipholus of Ephesus, and the two Dromios need to "go hand in hand, not one before another" (V.i.425), so that their image in the "glass" (V.i.417) is "chained" beside them, forced on their recognition, not comfortably allowed to face them in a medium which *seems* to relieve them of any real necessity of looking.

The characters in *The Comedy of Errors* are fundamentally incapable of seeing beyond the outward appearances which serve to complicate and confuse the management of their affairs. Although dimly aware of a need for identity and a need to face their problems on a deeper level than the one of mere external manifestation, they lack the power to pursue this need for they are, after all, little more than puppets at the mercy of a master manipulator. The real dramatic significance of their presentation, however, lies in the fact that each is presented with the adumbrations of a solution to his problem in the existence of his alter ego, and his inability to profit thereby is the result of powers as yet unrecognized, which blind him to the importance of the image in the glass.

Love's Labour's Lost

Love's Labour's Lost derives much of its permanent dramatic interest from the results of its characters' "unseeing." The academe which is set up right at the beginning of the play, whether it be called the pretentious "[school] of night" (IV.iii.254–55) or the more realistic "four woodcocks in a dish" (IV.iii.82), is a deliberate befuddling refusal to "see the merry days of / desolation" (I.ii.164–65) which the wilful reordering of life to fantastic notions of sophistication and sophistry will inevitably make the participants look upon. Whether Shakespeare is satirizing the Raleigh or Harvey coteries is really only incidentally dramatically relevant. The play's broad pattern is one of man's putative sophisticated veneer, of man's refusing to look into "the window of [his] heart" (V.ii.848), and it is delicious irony that it falls to the role of Costard the rustic and of the women to shatter the facade. Costard's punishment at the beginning of the play—"a year's imprisonment" (I.i.289) for being "taken with a wench" (I.i.290) —rebounds against the upholders of the academe's schedule "not to see a woman" (I.i.37) in their "three years' fast" (I.i.24) and also against their "own affections / And the huge army of the world's desires" (I.i.9–10), because this is almost exactly the punishment they themselves receive from the ladies—"A twelvemonth shall [they] spend, and never rest" (V.ii.831). At the very end of the play the

22

ladies set up the schedule of a fasting academy for the same four woodcocks which varies very little from the lords' own abortive schedule—"some forlorn and naked hermitage, / Remote from all the pleasures of the world" (V.ii.805–6) with the subtle distinction that they are now forcibly deprived of the society of the ladies by the ladies themselves, and made to undergo the fast as a trial of their love whether it be genuine and sincere or "made in heat of blood" (V.ii.810). The two songs with their postscript warning about the cuckoo mocking married men and the staring owl singing the "merry note" of "greasy Joan's" desolation are an ironical comment on the possible outcome of marriages "made in heat of blood."

The fame "that all hunt after in their lives" to make them "heirs of all eternity" (I.i.1,7) is not to be sought "while truth the while / Doth falsely blind the eyesight of [their] look[s]" (I.i.76). Biron all too eloquently points up how his "fellow-scholars" (I.i.17) "Climb o'er the house to unlock the little gate" (I.i.109), how the advent of the French King's daughter shows that their study has "quite forgot" (I.i.142) to face up to the reality of the present situation; how study "doth forget to do the thing it should; / And when it hath the thing it hunteth most, / 'Tis won as towns with fire, so won, so lost" (I.i.145–47) (which, ironically, is exactly what happens to all of them as a result of their course of study). Man cannot master the "affects" with which he is born "but by special grace" (I.i.153), and yet he subscribes to the thirty-nine articles of the academe's "protestation" (I.i.33) to find out "Things hid and barr'd" (I.i.57) by "study's god-like recompence" (I.i.58), forswearing himself on the mere necessity of believing that he is "the last that will last keep his oath" (I.i.161). What remarkable dramatic irony it is that the play shows us Biron breaking his oath before the other three and yet trying desperately to assert himself as the last when he is made to "see" the forswearing of the other three in sequence *after* his own fall.

Biron has the greatest potential for seeing through the stupidity of the academe's schedule and course of activity, and yet is caught out by his determination to show he is less of an ass than the rest. This is why it is most dramatically appropriate that his letter of love, his capitulation to forswearing, should go much further astray than the letters of his three fellow-scholars, and should be confused with Armado's letter to Jaquenetta by being entrusted to Costard to deliver. Biron's dramatic link with Armado and Costard is not just fortuitous. "How well he's read, to reason against reading!" (I.i.94), and yet what a "good l'envoy, ending in the goose" (III.i.101) he becomes to the other three, "The fox, the ape, and the humble-bee" (III.i.90).

Armado and Costard are to be used as the academe's "minstrelsy" (I.i.177) and "sport" (I.i.180) to make their three years' study "short" (I.i.181), but the scholars little realize how abruptly their course of study will be cut short by such a twain, or how ironically their use of Armado and Costard will afford an "umpire of their [own] mutiny" (I.i.170)—"against [their] own affections" (I.i.9). It takes a dull, stupid magistrate, to "reprehend" (I.i.184) the "Duke's own person" (I.i.182) in his arrest of Costard for being taken with a wench. His malapropish "rephrehend" for "represent" does appropriately end up reprehending the Duke for the stupidity of that item of the schedule which forbade "any man be seen to talk with a / woman within the term of three years" (I.i.130-1). On the other hand, Costard's malapropish remark that the "contempts" of the accusing letter "are as touching [him]" (I.i.191) does tend to indicate how the contents of the letter of accusation are

24

contemptuous of all those who would concur with the charge, for in "manner and form following" (I.i.207) it is "the manner of a man to speak to a woman . . . in some form . . . / As it shall follow in [their] correction" (I.i. 212,213,215). Costard does indeed "suffer for the truth" (I.i.313) which "Doth falsely blind the eyesight" (I.i.76) of his accusers' looks. What irony it is for the fellow-scholars to pass judgment on Costard and then set about "to put in practice that / Which each to other hath so strongly sworn" (I.i.308–9), and for them to begin this procedure by setting Armado as Costard's keeper. By the end of the play Costard impersonating Pompey the Big (shades of Fluellyn's Alexander the Pig) metaphorically whips Armado impersonating Hector with the news that Jaquenetta is "two months on her way" (V.ii.679), and then quite literally puts Armado to shame by successfully challenging him to fight in his shirt, a challenge which Armado in "naked truth" (V.ii.716) cannot accept. Armado has been made to see the "day of wrong through the little / hole of discretion" (V.ii.732–33). The three years which he promised to study with the Duke (I.ii.37–38) are now converted to the three years he has "vow'd to Jaquenetta to hold / the plough for her" (V.ii.892–93). He has been made to look upon his "merry days of desolation" and the staring owl hoots a merry note while the cuckoo "Mocks married men."

The fellow-scholars suffer a similar metamorphosis. They are not so much men "of fire-new words, fashion's own knight" (I.i.179) nor do they have Armado's peculiar "mint of phrases in [their] brain" (I.i.166), but they are most decidedly ravished by the "music of [their] own vain tongue" (I.i.167) pleading for their own virtues, unaware of the merry days of desolation which their actions are preparing for themselves ahead. How revealing of the group it is that the King has not only forgotten important state affairs that are immediately impending, namely the arrival of the French princess on embassy from her father, but has also lost all grip on state affairs of the past, having to confess to the princess's assurance of the payment of a debt that he "never heard of it" (II.i.158), but is willing to be satisfied on sight of acquittances which are forthcoming. The academe is apparently existing in a state of vacuum, but the day of retribution is beginning to shine through the academe's "eye, peeping thorough desire" (II.i.235). The academe's schedule is basically a last ditch defence against the invasion of love, though its scholars are hardly aware of it.

Armado's page, Moth, helps us to see through the holes in all the academicians' armor as well as in his master's. Armado may laugh at what he takes to be Costard's ignorant confusing of "l'envoy" and "salve," but Moth questions whether the wise think them any other than the same, and then plays the trick of having Armado who opened with a salve about the fox, the ape, and the humble-bee repeat Moth's envoy to it about the goose making a fourth so that Armado ends up by playing his own goose "Staying the odds by adding four" (III.i.99), and Costard is wise enough to remark that Moth has sold Armado a bargain "a goose, that's flat" (III.i.102). Costard also wisely "smell[s] some / l'envoy, some goose" (III.i.122–23) in Armado's decision to "enfranchise" him over the Jaquenetta affair, for the lorldly Latin remuneration of three farthings. Costard is enfranchised: Armado's freedom's gone.

Biron's remuneration to Costard for promising to commend to Rosaline's hand a "seal'd-up counsel" (III.i.170) is only "a 'leven-pence farthing better" (III.i.172) because "Some men must love my lady, and some Joan" (III.i.207).

26

Biron is acutely conscious of choosing "among three, to
love the worst of all" (III.i.197), but at least she is a lady,
whereas Armado is taken with "the country maid" (III.i.
131)—a greasy Joan, though the distinction tends to break
down somewhat when the Princess commands Boyet to
break the "neck of the wax" (IV.i.59) of the letter to
Jaquenetta knowing it to be mistaken for "a letter from
Monsieur Biron to one Lady Rosaline" (IV.i.53), and the
conversation takes a bawdy turn among the ladies, Boyet
and Costard to the extent that Maria accuses Costard of
talking "greasily" (IV.i.139) and Boyet dismisses Costard's
crudity "She's too hard for you at pricks, sir; challenge her
to bowl" (IV.i.140) by bidding Costard "Goodnight, my
good owl" (IV.i.141) because he fears "too much rubbing"
(IV.i.141). Costard can play the staring owl with a very
merry note. "Lord, Lord, how the ladies and [he] have
put . . . down" (IV.i.143) not so much Boyet, as first
Armado and second Biron, because it is, of course, their
love letters that Costard is carrying, and through them the
whole academe of the "Prince and his bookmates"
(IV.i.102). "When it comes so smoothly off, so obscenely,
as it were, so fit" (IV.i.145) it is a deliciously ironic
comment on how both Armado's and Biron's love affairs are
reduced to the common level of Costard's embassy, and is a
foretaste of Bottom's company rehearsing "most obscenely
and courageously" (*Dream*, I.ii.111) the "very tragical
mirth" (V.i.57) of the "tedious brief scene" (V.i.56) of the
lovers' involvements. Indeed the "words of Mercury [the
messenger—Costard reducing things to real life consider-
ations] are harsh after / the songs of Apollo" (the god of
inspiration for letters, blinding in his own brilliance)
(V.ii.940–41).

How remarkably dramatically appropriate it is that
Costard should then deliver Biron's letter to Jaquenetta,

27

and accompany her to master Parson Nathaniel to have it read—whose "ignorance were wise, / Where now his knowledge must prove ignorance" (II.i.102–3). Nathaniel has just been begging master schoolmaster Holofernes to "abrogate scurrility" (IV.ii.56), which is a timely comment on Dull's argument with the two "book-men" (IV.ii.35) about the nature of the deer the Princess has struck. Holofernes with his "haud credo" doubts whether the deer be a "buck of the first head" (IV.ii.10) or a buck of the second, namely a "pricket" as Nathaniel is assured, but Dull affirms no amount of "collusion" between the two Latin academics or their "pollusion" of terms can really confuse the issue. They cannot deny that the moon can never be more than four weeks old. Dull's posing of the moon riddle to the two bookmen is roughly equivalent to Moth's forcing the goose envoy on Armado, and it has further significance in that the "allusion holds in the exchange" (IV.ii.42) in the sense that the deer that the Princess has slain is, of course, the Prince, and in the sense that the Prince is no longer lasting than the other members of the academe in his defence against love's arrows; he is certainly not so much a wily experienced buck of the first head as an easy victim of the second.

That Biron's love letter to Rosaline should be read by Nathaniel and listened to by Holofernes for its "apostrophas" and poetical "accent" and found lacking in the "golden cadence of poesy" (IV.ii.126) because it fell short of Ovid is at one level a dull academic indictment against the academe inviting an obvious comparison with the stultified "Absey book" (*King John* I.i.196) rhetoric letter of Armado, but on another is an ironic comment on the academe's profession of love "never going aright" (III.i.194) least of all for Biron.

And the *series* of love letters? Each of the scholars is

shattered by having to write a love letter and seeing the consequences of that shattering by watching the next victim's antics. This, I suggest, is the real purpose behind the somewhat artificial business of having first the King, then Longaville, then Dumain read their love letters, overheard by ever increasing numbers—it is the cumulative mirror effect that is being striven for. The dramatis personae themselves are only vaguely aware of the shattering effects of love—they see themselves at one, two, and three removes. The King may exclaim "My tears for glasses" (IV.iii.39) in his love sonnet, but it is merely the "golden cadency of poesy" in that tears figure differently and each time more eloquently in everyone of his sonnet expressions making him beautifully transparent; he even adds an extra couplet to his sonnet as if to reinforce its poetic formality. At least only Biron overheard the King, and thus the King's dignity is asserted at the expense of the wittiest of the four woodcocks. Longaville's "heavenly rhetoric" sonnet, seeking to justify its author in that he forswore woman not a goddess, certainly "makes flesh a deity, / A green goose a goddess" (IV.iii.74–75). Longaville, like Armado, has been sold a bargain "a goose, that's flat" (III.i.102), and Biron noticing it is really looking at his own image. He is certainly not the "demigod" he imagines himself to be sitting in the sky heedfully o'er-eying "wretched fools' secrets" (IV.iii.80) like a Puck, nor is he like a Costard with his "Lord, Lord, how the ladies and I have put [them] down" (IV.i.143). Dumain's ode seeks to excuse his author on the grounds that Jove himself would "deny himself for Jove / Turning mortal" (IV.iii.119–20) for the love of "most divine Kate" (IV.iii.83)—"For none offend where all alike do dote" (IV.iii.126)—and the whole series has run to its logical conclusion. All there remains is for the series to rewind itself with Longaville accusing Dumain, the King Longaville, and Biron the King—"a king transformed to a gnat" (IV.iii.166)—until all things are wound up in Biron himself, who is brought face to face with Costard and Jaquenetta delivering to the King his love letter, which has already been read aloud by the pedants and now has to be scrutinized by his fellow scholars in the light of his severe comments on their letters. In vain does Biron try to tear up his disgrace. How dramatically appropriate it is that the fragmented Biron is picked up from the floor, reassembled, and added as the envoy, the goose, to the other three's salve—"That you three fools lack'd me fool to make up the mess" (IV.iii.207). Costard's remark, "Walk aside the true folk, and let the traitors stay" (IV.iii.213), is ironically poignant.

And after the scholars are unmasked as lovers it is powerfully ironic that they should hit on the idea of masking themselves from the ladies' worlds in the vizards of Muscovites, and very appropriate that just when they are emerging into what they hope is to be the spring and summer of delights they are hoodwinked by the masqued ladies who deliberately exchange the favors bestowed on them by the Prince and his bookmates, and thus destroy the only basis the lover has for recognizing "his several mistress" (V.ii.124).

The academe has "liv'd long on the almsbasket / of words" (V.i.41–42), has proceeded no further than the elementary lesson in the alphabet of love. Moth schooling Holofernes affords a cruel parallel. Holofernes for all his great learning is quizzed by Moth first on the significance of the reversal of the first two letters of the alphabet and then on the elementary order of the vowels so that whether Holofernes pronounce the third vowel himself ("I") or have Moth pronounce the fifth ("U-You") there is no escaping the fact that Holofernes has been sold "a [ba>sheep], that's flat" (III.i.102). No wonder Costard is so pleased as to wish Moth were his bastard, for Moth has reduced the pedants, and through them the Prince and his bookmates, to the dunghill of their own fingers' ends—the scraps of a great feast.

Armado's coming to Holofernes and Nathaniel to "crave [their] / assistance" (V.i.122–23) in presenting "the Princess, sweet chuck, with some delightful / ostentation, or show, or pageant, or antic, or fire- / work" (V.i.117–19) reduces the academe to the scraps of its own intelligence. In looking at the show of the "Nine Worthies" (V.i.130) muddled through as it is by Costard, Dull, Moth, Holofernes, Armado, and Nathaniel, they are looking at mocking representations of themselves. Armado presenting Hector of Troy has to "play the honest Troyan" (V.ii.681) and be metaphorically "whipp'd for Jaque / netta that is quick by him" (V.ii.686–87)—just so the academe, "brave conquerors . . . That war against [their] own affections / And the huge army of the world's desires" (I.i.8,9–10), has to play the honest Trojan and be whipped by Cupid. Costard presenting Pompey the Great laying his "arms before the legs of this sweet lass of France" (V.ii.558) is a far too close parallel for the King not to feel "shame" (V.ii.512). Nathaniel presenting the world conqueror Alexander—"fame, that all hunt after in their lives" (I.i.1), "dismay'd" (V.ii.570) and shoved to one side, "scrap'd out of the painted cloth" (V.ii.579) closely parallels the academe's putting on one side its aspiration of having fame "Live regist'red upon [its] brazen tombs" (I.i.2). Moth presenting the labors of Hercules "in minority" (V.ii.596) makes nonsense of the academe's labors to make "Navarre . . . the wonder of the world" (I.i.12). Holofernes, the supreme Jud-as (V.ii.631)-headed pedant, playing, Bottom-like, three worthies pedantically all in one is stripped of his pretentions to the greatness

31

of a Maccabaeus—"Judas Maccabaeus clipt is plain Judas" (V.ii.603) and reduced to the "kissing traitor" (V.ii.604), furnishing a powerful comment on how the academe itself has proved a traitor to its lofty schedule.

The spectators are all gathered together watching the nine un-worthies but, of course, they do not recognize themselves in this tedious brief scene of their own love's labor's lost. The Princess may argue like Theseus in *A Midsummer Night's Dream* after her that the play put on by the rude mechanicals

> best pleases that doth [least] know how;
> Where zeal strives to content, and the contents
> Dies in the zeal of that which it presents. (V.ii.517–19)

but what an ironic comment it is on them all to conclude

> Their form confounded makes most form in mirth,
> When great things labouring perish in their birth.
> (V.ii.520–21)

Biron little realizes in his applauding this description by the Princess of the show of the Nine Worthies "A right description of our sport, my lord" (V.ii.522) that it is indeed a right description of the sport the academe has been providing through "the window of [its] heart" (V.ii.848) into its *Love's Labour's Lost*.

Love's Labour's Lost represents not so much man's desire to rise above the level of his base humanity as his refusal to admit that his humanity exists. The futility of attempting to substitute the thin veneer of scholarly and sophisticated dedication for the solid worth of a little practical government and a little self-knowledge is demonstrated forcibly as each of the four deluded men faces the evidence of all too obviously human frailty. Finally each one is presented with the proof not only of his own failure to change his image but also of the crumbling of his ideals, which lacked sufficient substance and depth of forethought. As in *The Comedy of Errors* the characters are offered the opportunity to look into the mirror of themselves, to see themselves for what they are and learn to live with the reality, but they are totally unable to accept the underlying meaning of the lesson and their appreciative applause for the outward performance effectively shatters the briefly offered glass with its unwelcome insight into matters more conveniently left hidden.

The Two Gentlemen of Verona

The Two Gentlemen of Verona begins to exploit the protean situations love will put man through in his quest for true, unMuscovited, unvizarded, and unshamable love. "Who is Silvia? What is she," the delicious touchstone lyric of the play, is deliberately enigmatical. Who is Silvia? What is she? She is really Julia to Proteus, when, his protean journey over and unmasked in the green woods' episode (a foretaste of many such episodes to follow in Shakespeare), he apparently recognizes his true love, his "wish for ever" (V.iv.119). She is Silvia when in his sea-change into something not rich but certainly strange he is foresworn to Valentine, Thurio, the Duke, and more importantly to himself, in the wooing of her.

Proteus at the very beginning of the play is accused by Valentine of being a "votary to fond desire" (I.i.52) his "wit by folly vanquished" (I.i.35), and Proteus, despite his witty answers and agreement that Julia has "metamorphos'd" him to such an extent that he does "neglect [his] studies" (I.i.67), shows too much interest in Valentine's travel, and is quick to answer Speed's witty suggestion that Speed has "play'd the sheep in losing" (I.i.73) Valentine, by his reassertion of the master-servant relationship on the basis of the remuneration the master pays to the servant for the servant's services. Speed is right to say that "Such another proof will make [him] cry 'baa'" (I.i.97), because

34

like Moth he has sold the master-servant relationship a green goose.

Speed has lost his silly sheep of a master Valentine, and Proteus in championing Valentine's course of action as being that of a shepherd not a silly sheep is making his own course that of a silly sheep. To Proteus's question whether Speed has given Proteus's letter to Julia, Speed, assuming the role of the lost sheep but adding to it implications of a love that is *bought* by changing the phrase to "lost mutton," and thus throwing Proteus's remuneration theme back at him, makes a noddy fool of Proteus. Proteus is made to "take [.] the pains to set" (I.i.123) "nod" and "Ay" together, and then be stuck with it, and this is especially appropriate after Proteus has been made to open his purse and pay for being made a noddy, and criticized for not carrying "[his] letters [him]self" (I.i.154).

In this last is the crux of the whole of the first scene and one of the main considerations for the whole play. Proteus in not being his own ambassador of love and further in using Valentine's servant and not his own to carry his letters to Julia is basically trying to cover up for the fact that his attachment to Julia is a hindrance to his desire "To see the wonders of the world abroad" (I.i.6). Valentine in this sense is his real self to whom he is so artificially saying goodbye, but he would be the first to deny it. His love-book for Julia is truly a "shallow story of deep love" (I.i.21).

Like Julia we "would [we] knew his mind" (I.ii.33), but unlike Julia we are not metamorphosed by the receipt of a letter from Proteus the contents of which Lucetta knows will resolve Julia of her forced difficulty of which of the three gentlemen—"fair Sir Eglamour . . . rich Mercatio . . . gentle Proteus" (I.ii.9,12,14)—to fall in love with. With Lucetta we are already concerned that Julia "stumble not unheedfully" (I.ii.3) and not cast her love away, for "Lord, Lord! to see what folly reigns in us!" (I.ii.15). Julia will not read the letter and yet has to do penance in calling Lucetta back for a second chance. Proteus will not at this stage accompany Valentine to Milan and yet will have to suffer for his renunciation.

And what delicious irony it is that Julia having accused Lucetta of receiving not a letter from Proteus but from "Some love of [hers] hath writ to [her] in rhyme" (I.ii.79) should be told by Lucetta that her ladyship must set the tune for her servant, and what irony for that tune to be fixed by Julia as "Light o' love" (I.ii.83). Julia can emerge from music's duel as triumphant provided she adheres to the idea that the letter is from a light lover of Lucetta's, and thus Proteus has an opportunity to escape from prisoner's base, but in tearing up Proteus's letter Julia is for ever letting thoughts of him tear her heart to pieces and will never be whole again till he be hers. No wonder all she has to say at the end of the play is that in having Proteus she has her wish for ever. Like Lucetta she can fall back on her femininity and simply plead that she has "no other but a woman's reason" (I.ii.23).

Proteus's protestation of love to Julia is aptly represented by the torn letter at the beginning of the play and ironically by the letter he has Julia disguised as Sebastian deliver to Silvia only to be torn up (IV.iv.136). The fragmented Proteus lying in pieces on the floor has to be assembled not only by Julia for "no other but a woman's reason," but also by the audience. He is exceedingly difficult to put back together again without "woman's reason." And Proteus's own efforts to be understood "drench[.] [him] in the sea, where [he is] drown'd" (I.iii.79), for he declares to his father, who for a month has been hammering at his son for "Not being tried and tutor'd in the world" (I.iii.21), that the letter he is reading is "a word or two / Of commendations sent from Valentine" (I.iii.52–53) because he fears to show his father Julia's letter "Lest he should take exceptions to [his] love" (I.iii.81). On a very superficial level he knows that he himself has provided his father with objections to his "love," but much more significantly he does not realize that the terms of the excuse, supplanting Julia by Valentine, point to the fundamental state of his wishes. That is why he can say his "heart accords" (I.iii.90) to his father's resolve that he shall "spend some time / With Valentinus in the Emperor's court" (I.iii.66–67), *before* he voices the lover's objections to being separated from his loved one—"And yet a thousand times it answers 'no' " (I.iii.91).

What irony it is that Proteus, like Antipholus of Syracuse, mentally trying to escape from love's chain, should be anchoring his sea change on Valentine when Valentine on reaching Milan is himself immediately "metamorphos'd with a mistress" (II.i.31) to such an extent that his mistress has him writing love letters "Unto the secret nameless friend of [hers]" (II.i.111) without Valentine's realizing that she is her own "nameless friend." Nor will Valentine even begin to understand despite his servant Speed's trying to shepherd his silly sheep of a master in the right direction that "Herself hath taught her love himself to write unto her lover" (II.i.174). Valentine has truly written the letters as if he were someone else. He is adrift on a sea of his own choosing and blind to its very tides. And it is on this very same sea that Proteus is now setting forth bidding his love adieu in such eloquence that even he is aware how badly it compares with the silence of Julia's "true love" (II.ii.17).

Launce's castigation of Proteus's emotionless parting with Julia is appropriately and specifically memorable for the detail that the cat was "wringing her hands" (II.iii.8)

37

—Julia's "tide of tears" (II.ii.14)—while the "cruel-hearted cur" (II.iii.10)—Proteus—shed not one tear, there being "no more pity in him than a dog" (II.iii.11). Proteus is only too anxious to get away from being "tied" (II.ii.14, 15; II.iii.40–44,56), and yet he is going to join a Valentine who has now been reduced to making his "wit bankrupt" (II.iv.42) by bandying words with the foolish Thurio and made to feel the necessity of praising Proteus to the Duke for "his experience old" (II.iv.69) and "his judgement ripe" (II.iv.70) whereas earlier these were the very qualities Valentine accused Proteus of not having.

The change in attitude has been brought about because Valentine has now found that "his mistress / . . . hold[s] his eyes lock'd in her crystal looks" (II.iv.88–89), and now indeed Valentine can say of Proteus that he "knew him as [him]self" (II.iv.62). In fact for much of the play Valentine is very subordinate to Proteus and to such an extent at times that he is best looked at as a guiding foil to him. One thing that perhaps causes us difficulty with this interpretation is that Valentine becomes interesting in and for himself, and Shakespeare does not resist putting Valentine through protean changes too, making him fall in love with the idea of Silvia—Speed reminds him that he "never saw her since she was deform'd" (II.i.68)—for love does not *see* its loved object but the object it has metamorphosed its loved one into. Shakespeare does not make the same mistake over Silvia. Surely it is idle for criticis to comment adversely on Silvia's impassively standing by at the end of the play—no other role would suit the dramatist's purposes anything like so well. "Who is Silvia? What is she, / That *all* [the] swains commend her?" She is a figment of Proteus's imagination, that quite impossible she. Julia by contrast is too obtainable.

Valentine, of course, seeks to make Proteus *his* foil and

to have Julia "dignified with [the] high honour / To bear [his] lady's train" (II.iv.158–59), but the "ladder made of cords" (II.iv.182) whereby he is to attain the summit of his expectations with his "betroth'd" Silvia is undone step by step by Proteus's need to "prove constant to [him]self" (II.vi.31) in his infatuation with Silvia, though by thus wronging his friend he will be as much forsworn as his servant-self Launce declares Speed will be for welcoming Launce to Milan (II.v.2). Despite Proteus's long soliloquies which certainly afford us with some of the play's most powerful writing (I.iii.78–87; II.iv.191–214; II.vi.1– 43) it is still true in Lucetta's reply to Julia's decision to "undertake / A journey to [her] loving Proteus" (II.vii.6–7) that "the way is wearisome and long" (II.vii.8). In *The Comedy of Errors* and *Love's Labour's Lost* the various protean stances in which man's vision of himself is temporarily shattered eventually lead to a promise of re-estimation on the basis of time's maturing, penance and fasting. But ironically in *The Two Gentlemen of Verona* only Valentine tends to follow this pattern and he is not the play's main concern. With Proteus the multiple fragmentation in the form of many couples reflecting similar situations is telescoped more or less into one person, and that person is beginning to look introspectively into himself, but he does not understand what he sees.

Although Proteus recognizes the necessity to "check [his] erring love" (II.iv.213) if at all possible, he allows himself to drown in self-pursuits, basically in self love like Narcissus considering that "love is still most precious in itself" (II.vi.24) when centered on itself, for he is dearer to himself than to any friend and must needs therefore be foresworn to others in order to "prove constant to [him]-self" (II.vi.31). As Launce remarks, Proteus is "a kind of a knave" (III.i.262), and again in Launce's words—

39

"but / that's all one, if he be but one knave" (III.i.262–63) an impossible state of affairs since he is *Proteus,* but all the knaves of Shakespeare who follow him owe him some debt though he be but a pale shadow of their substance.

It is as if Proteus in his soliloquies, however, were merely going through the motions of examining his conscience in much the same way as he goes through the motions of evaluating his love for Julia—both are protean stances. The way to Proteus "is wearisome and long." Who is Proteus? What is he that Julia so exalts him as to make her pilgrimage like "The current that with gentle murmur glides . . . in his pilgrimage . . . to the wild ocean" (II.vii.25,30,32) to "such divine perfection" (II.vii.13). Lucetta correctly chides that the thousand oaths, oceans of tears, and instances of infinite love which her mistress claims warrant her welcome to Proteus "are servants to deceitful men" (II.vii.72). Julia must needs wear a "codpiece" (II.vii.53) in her pilgrimage attire if she is to be realistic.

And what a situation there is in the shrine itself. Proteus's betraying of Valentine's plan to the Duke; Proteus's responsibility for Valentine's banishment; Proteus's wooing of Silvia for himself—all are catechised by his servant's catechism of his own milk-maid love (III.i.265–77) that wealth will cover a multitude of deficiencies and even make "the faults / gracious" (III.i.377–78). Silvia's wealth as the Duke's daughter will make up for Proteus's illegal means to gain it. And yet Proteus is to be fobbed off with only the picture of Silvia hanging in her chamber "For since the substance of [her] perfect self / Is else devoted, [he is] but a shadow; / And to [her] shadow will [he] make true love" (IV.ii.124–26), for which he is prepared to pay Julia's ring.

What irony it is that Julia now disguised as Sebastian is

employed by Proteus to deliver the ring to Silvia and for this mission to be made tolerable to Julia only because of her recognition that if Proteus were assured of Silvia herself and not just her portrait he "would, sure, deceive it, / And make it but a shadow, as [she is] (IV.ii.127–28). Proteus is indeed worshipping shadows and adoring false shapes (IV.iv.131) mostly of his own casting. Proteus is not made to think in terms of true love until Valentine (love tested by the adversity of unlooked for banishment— Proteus's banishment from Julia had after all been wishful) shatters the last and worst of Proteus's stances, his own bestiality desecrating the object it was supposed to adore (this, I think, is the significance of Launce's long description of his dog's heaving up its leg and making water against Silvia's farthingale) (IV.iv.40–41). The issue is successfully forced upon him by Valentine. No wonder Valentine's line, "All that was mine in Silvia I give thee" (V.iv.83), addressed to Proteus causes us difficulty at first. It is brilliantly shocking. It makes Proteus pick up the fragments of his shadowy letter himself. In the full glare of being *given* his cherished object the shadows fall away and he can really *see* not Silvia but Silvia in Julia.

What is Silvia? What is she but Julia to "a constant eye" (V.iv.115). It is, of course, to be hoped that Proteus like the banished men who sheltered his Valentine self in the wild wood of his own bestial banishment can be forgiven by everyone as well as by Julia, though by no means so easily, on the understanding that like them he is "reformed, civil, full of good, / And fit for great employment" (V.iv.156–57).

In *The Two Gentlemen of Verona* Proteus and to a lesser extent Valentine suffer the fragmentation of self into the components necessary for self-analysis, but neither is willing or able to understand what he sees. Proteus is dimly aware of his reprehensible conduct and a vague need to reform his ways, but self-love and the pursuit of his own interests blind him to the discomforting image in the glass of introspection. For Valentine there is at least some promise of an enforced re-estimation of self through his banishment, but for Proteus the glimpse of reality is so far obscured by the need to gain his own ends that even the real Julia and the real Silvia are lost to him. His protean mind is so unwilling to face facts that it conveniently distorts the truth before it into the fiction of his own desires and endows Julia with the attributes he sought in Silvia. The image in the glass is much too uncomfortable to live with and must be shattered irrevocably if Proteus is to pursue his own blind and selfish happiness as before.

The Taming of the Shrew

Who is Bianca? What is she that all the swains commend *her* and avoid Katherina? Is not *she* the shrew whose "silence flouts" (II.i.29) us, whose dilly-dallying with suitors—"Fair Leda's daughter had a thousand wooers" (I.ii.244)—not telling whom she loves best (II.i.9), whose assertion that we do her "double wrong / To strive for that which resteth in [her] choice" (III.i.16–17), who casts her "wand'ring eyes on every stale" (III.i.90), who literally has to supply "her sister's room" (III.ii.252) at the wedding banquet, but possibly has been metaphorically doing so all the time, who doubts that a "taming-school" exists (IV.ii.55), whose love causes her suitors to resort to subterfuge and to disguise themselves in menial ranks and run the risk of someone who believes in being just herself, in calling a spade a spade, breaking the false situation over the transformed lover's head, who *demands* that men come to her not she to them, who scolds her Lucentio for laying a bet on her "duty" (V.ii.129), whose hand is to go to the highest bidder, and who is summed up brilliantly by Petruchio as a drawn blank—for Hortensio with his widow and Lucentio with Bianca have "hit the white" (V.ii.186).

Kate reminds Hortensio, who looks for the "gentler, milder mould" (I.i.60) of Bianca, that this outward semblance is "not half way to her heart" (I.i.62), and even if it were it would not prevent Bianca from combing his "noddle

43

with a three-legg'd stool" (I.i.64) and making a milksop out of him by painting his face and generally using him "like a fool" (I.i.65).

Bianca is really "the ground of all [dis]cord" (III.i.73), the main connection between plot and subplot, to be excused only by laying some of the charges at her father's door for preferring this "treasure" (II.i.32) of his younger daughter's apparent meek submissiveness (the mewing image, I.i.87), because she is "apt to learn and thankful for good turns" (II.i.166), to the vigorous independent spirit of Kate. No wonder Petruchio's job of taming Kate is of whirlwind progress and practically a foregone conclusion. The "lusty wench" (II.i.161) that can reduce Hortensio to the state of a "pillory, looking through the lute" (II.i.157) puts up little more than a token show of resistance to Petruchio only. There are many times when she could volubly resist Petruchio's "taming" and give him the "penance of her tongue" (I.i.89) if she so desired, but her "silence flouts" (II.i.29) the shrew image, and Petruchio's "If she be curst, it is for policy" (II.i.294) has more truth in it, perhaps, than even Petruchio realizes at the time. His suggestion that he and Kate have bargained between themselves alone that although "she shall still be curst in company" (II.i.307) it is "incredible to believe / How much she loves [him]" (II.i.308-9) is a great deal more than bravado. Kate's "shrewishness" is thus for public show, a way of countering her lack of attention and protecting against the "meacock wretch[es]" (II.i.315) who can all too easily "make the curstest shrew." Kate's fear is obviously lest as an old maid she "lead apes in hell" (II.i.34), but much more significantly, I suggest, that if she does not rebel against all that Baptista and Bianca stand for she will *end* up being a shrew and not marrying someone who has more than a look of a real lord and master about him.

The first taming, a wild battle of wits, assures her that she has met a fire as great as her own (II.i.133), but it may be Petruchio who is being tested, too. Kate's charge that he "thinks with oaths to face the matter out" (II.i.291) elicits real *action* by the promise in front of her father and other witnesses to marry her "upon Sunday" (II.i.300), and to Petruchio's claim that she is only a shrew in public "[t]he lady protests too much" in answering nothing. Although she is denied the pomp and circumstance of a wedding, of a banquet feast, of having a handsomely decked bridegroom, of luscious foods, of costly raiment, these things hardly affect her because she is not won with such trivialities.

The deprivation of her marriage rights reported by Curtis (IV.i.186) makes her sit "as one new-risen from a dream" (IV.i.189). But what was her dream? Was she allowing Petruchio his victories because they were what she wanted too, but now must play the more subtle game of allowing her husband to *think* that he is taming her? How else can we explain the effectiveness of Petruchio's threat not to "return unto [her] father's house" (IV.iii.53) on her? To go back to her father's house must be the last thing to be desired at this stage of the game. It is obviously true that *later* she revels at home in lording it over her sister and the widow, laying the "serve, love, and obey" (V.ii.164) catechism on so thickly and at such length. She plays Petruchio's idiot boy game of calling the sun the moon, and outvies Petruchio's description of Vincentio as a "Fair lovely maid" worthy to be embraced "for her beauty's sake" (IV.v.33–34) by calling him a "Young budding virgin, fair and fresh and sweet" (IV.v.37) who would make a man very happy to have her "for his lovely bed-fellow!" (IV.v.-41). Kate gets her man and encourages the master look of him. Petruchio understands the situation and since the dower is assuredly adequate is pleased to be understood.

45

But the sly question we all ask with Christopher as with Antipholus of Syracuse is "Am I a lord? And have I such a lady? / Or do I dream? Or have I dream'd till now?" (Induction ii.70–71).

Sly, bullied by the Hostess and disallowed to take his ease in his inn, escapes in sleep and is *literally* possessed by a "flatt'ring dream or worthless fancy" (Induction i.44) laid on at the instigation of the Oberon-like hunting lord. All the "wanton pictures" (Induction i.47) of the lustful beds of Cytherea, Jove, and Apollo do not succeed in seducing sly Christopher to consider the "lady" anything more than "Madam wife" (Induction ii.114) or his drink anything more than "a poto' th' smallest ale" (Induction ii.77), but then if they want him to believe he has been in a dream "These fifteen years" (ii.81) there is no harm in seeing what present benefits are to be derived from awaking—hence the immediate instructions to the "lady" to undress and "come now to bed" (ii.119), a sequence which is skilfully paralleled by the play's ending too! When this move is frustrated with the excuse that the physicians have expressly charged that the lady should absent herself from the felicity of her lord's bed awhile lest this incur his "former malady" (ii.124) Christopher, "loath to fall into [his] dreams again" (ii.128–29), tarries "in despite of the flesh / and the blood" (ii.129) to "let the world slip" (ii.146) and watches the first entanglements of love's metamorphoses with Lucentio suffering the effects of "love in idleness" (I.i.156), burning, pining, perishing—the very subject of wanton seduction the lord had tried to make of *him*. Lucentio sees sweet beauty in Bianca's face "Such as the daugher of Agenor had, / That made great Jove to humble him to her hand, / When with his knees he kiss'd the Cretan strand" (I.i.173–75), and *humbles* himself to be a "schoolmaster / And undertake the teaching of the maid" (I.i.196–97), allowing Tranio to take his place as master and thereby ironically extending the meaning of "Nor can we be distinguish'd by our faces / For man or master" (I.i.205–6). This is *The Comedy of Errors* with a seduced difference. Lucentio's excuse to his other servant, Biondello, that he has "kill'd a man" and fears he "was descried" (I.i.237) is double-edged too in that by following this course of action consequent on love in idleness Lucentio has killed his own mastership and manhood, and, as the end of the play shows, he has drawn a blank.

The sight of Lucentio's madness has the excellent effect of sending Christopher back into his dreams again— Lucentio's action is a "very excellent piece of work. . . . would 'twere done!" (I.i.258–59)—and it may not be purely coincidental that the moment Christopher fades out of the play Petruchio bounces in. It seems to me entirely possible that just as one and the same actor can play both Christopher and Petruchio so we are dramatically within rights in suggesting that Petruchio is Sly's dream self, and Lucentio the dream self he knows others would force on him.

Sly is crafty enough to know that it is milksop Lucentio-Hortensio weaklings that duly get the shrews their actions have so busily been creating for themselves, and also to know that a good "lusty wench" with independent spirit can only be achieved by meeting fire with fire and coming to some private arrangement with her. His dream self is apparently capable of doing it, but even in this dream world his Petruchio and Lucentio selves keep crossing each other's paths, though he feels superior enough over Lucentio to be able to stand aside and watch the subplotting antics of Lucentio.

Sly is looking at himself through a dream mirror and watching a "kind of history" (Induction ii.144) of "mirth

47

and merriment" (ii.137) which sees himself as devoid of the frenzy of melancholy, and not just letting the world slip by without giving it one or two hearty slaps in its convention-ridden aspects to the amazement of the cuffed priest and the besopped-faced sexton (III.ii.165,175).

The Taming of the Shrew offers a study not of self-delusion but rather of self-disguise deliberately used in the attainment of one's ends. Both Kate and Bianca have seemingly looked into the glass and recognized themselves for what they are but deem their real natures unconducive to success in the matters that concern them. Consequently Bianca prefers to mask her truly shrewish disposition with the outward semblance of meek submissiveness while Kate uses her reputation for shrewishness as a powerful weapon in warding off an unwelcome suitor. When Kate has won Petruchio and found him to have a spirit equal to her own she no longer needs to deny the revelation of her true character in his presence and reserves the outward veneer of fierce independence for mere public show. Bianca on the other hand is now free to give full rein to the private sharpening of her wits at the expense of the poor meek Lucentio. For Christopher Sly all this is a convenient escape into a dream world where he, a meek and mild person, can vicariously enjoy the vigorous brashness of his desirable alter ego, Petruchio.

A Midsummer Night's Dream

A Midsummer Night's Dream, weaving together as it does the earlier comedies, reaches a remarkable peak of dramatic development. *The Comedy of Errors* is present in the carefully manipulated series of mistaken identities based partly on the Athenian garments mix up by Puck, but more particularly on the fact that on the mere potioning of the eye he who was formerly in love with the little dark-haired Hermia suddenly declares in the name of reason he is in love with the tall fair-haired maypole Helena; and she who declared herself divorced from Oberon's bed finds herself in love with translated Bottom, on a bed "where the wild thyme blows" (II.i.249) and the woodbine hangs on the eglantine. That affections should be so visually manipulated. *Love's Labour's Lost* is most assuredly present in that all the lovers watch the lamentable tragedy of the tedious brief scene of Pyramus and Thisbe without seeing the lamentable tragedy and tedious briefness of their own love situations.

Theseus may in his own mind be setting up an academy in which reason shall prevail—his relationship with Hippolyta is free from the violent heady passions of frantic love in all its comedy of errors and protean changes, but there are many indications that his imagining this is *love* is his midsummer night's dream. In point of fact Hippolyta is really his latest *conquest,* and his attitude toward her is that of a conqueror on equal military terms (for she is an Amazon), not that of a lover over feminine weakness. His whole attempt to present her with "pomp, with triumph, and with revelling" (I.i.19) dreaming away the time until the nuptial hour is to while away this intervening time until he can make the final conquest. Stirring up the "Athenian youth to merriments" (I.i.12) is his equivalent of the King of Navarre's use of Armado. And the entertainment—"the headie force of frentick love" which Hippolyta calls "'the silliest stuff that ever [she] heard" (V.i.212)—mocks Theseus's intended marriage. No emotional headiness, no feminine weakness, but an addiction to manly sports—the sounds of the hunt in particular of which she says she never "heard / So musical a discord, such sweet thunder" (IV.i.121–22)—spells a rather awkward kind of marriage, and even Bottom's remark that "reason and love keep little company together now- / a-days" (III.i.147–48) is a relevant criticism of Theseus's situation.

Theseus may think he is being rational: the lack of success of his entertainment argues that his labor of "love" is lost. Even Bottom, the hempen home-spun rudest mechanical out-malaproping Costard and out-dulling Dull, is vouchsafed a vision of the Queen of Fairies, but like sly old Christopher never loses his plebian sense of the taste of hay, spurning thereby all ultra delicacies, and like preeminently Petruchio knows the value of monetary rewards—"sixpence a day during his life . . . for playing Pyramus" (IV.ii.20–22), translated though he may have been in his behind the bush unguarded moments.

Theseus in delivering Hermia over to her father Egeus's ruling that she should marry Demetrius, the man of *his* choice, and not Lysander, the man of hers, conveniently forgets that Demetrius was "betroth'd" (IV.i.176) to

A Midsummer Night's Dream

Helena "ere [he] saw Hermia." One is reminded of the King of Navarre's convenient lapse of memory about the coming of the "admir'd princess" (I.i.141) which makes it necessary for the King himself to break the academy's rule that no man shall "be seen to talk with a / woman within the term of three years" (I.i.130–31). The very rules of reason, order, and obedience which both Theseus and the King of Navarre set up are broken down almost immediately by their own actions. The pre-contract between Helena and Demetrius is restored by love-in-idleness—"the headie force of frentick love." Demetrius's love pattern has moved from one protean extreme to the other and back again, and he can laugh a Pyramus and Thisbe and not see himself in them.

The Two Gentlemen of Verona is present in Lysander and Demetrius, the former paralleling Valentine, the latter Proteus. Demetrius abandons Helena and pursues Lysander's loved one Hermia: Lysander under the influence of love-in-idleness in the green woods abandons Hermia to Demetrius and pursues Demetrius's loving one, Helena. "Lord, what fools these [gentlemen] be!" (III.ii.115) would be a ripe comment. Who is Hermia; what is she that both the swains commend her one minute, and who is Helena; what is she that the same two swains commend her the next? Demetrius and Lysander fall over themselves to hand over their loved one to their rival—"All that was mine in [Hermia / Helena] I give thee" (V.iv.83).

There is unmistakably in Hermia something of the shrew as Helena's remarks about her to the men reveal. She is a vixen who with her sharp tongue and nails terrifies Helena, but it is Helena over whom the two men are metamorphosed and are prepared to fight a duel in the woods, lost as they are in the maze of their frantic passions, misled by their puckish intentions, and it is Helena who is rewarded

51

in the end by having Demetrius's violent affection return to her uncorrected by the chastening force of "Dian's bud" (IV.i.76), whereas Hermia has her lover's passion returned, duly chastened. The "spotted snakes with double tongue" (II.ii.9) which Titania's boudoir fairies try to exorcise from her bed are metaphorically realized not just for Titania in the Bottom-ass cuckolding episode (which in many senses is not simply Titania's degradation only, because it reflects satirically on Oberon, as the parallel crowning of Bottom and the Indian boy with flowers from the bridal bed makes clear), but also for Hermia in her dream of a "crawling serpent" (II.ii.146,149) eating her heart away, and in her false accusation of Demetrius as a serpent for having killed her Lysander sleeping, than whom "never adder stung" indeed "with doubler tongue" (III.ii.73,72).

Oberon's "taming" of Titania obviously suggests a Petruchio-Katherina parallel, but what a subtle difference there is. The dwarf King of fairies, the "king of shadows" (III.ii.347), motivates the whole "fierce vexation of a [midsummer night's] dream" (IV.i.72), because he demands Titania hand over the changeling Indian boy, son of a votaress of Titania's "order" (II.i.123) to be his "henchman" (II.i.121), "Knight of his train, to trace the forests wild" (II.i.25). The whole eye potioning business, the "distemperature" (II.i.106) of the seasons in which "rheumatic diseases do abound" (II.i.105) and in which "hot ice and wondrous strange snow" (V.i.59)—Theseus's comment at the end of the play—mark the discord of debate and dissension—"this progeny of evils" (II.i.115) springs from the dispute between Oberon and Titania.

But the dispute is not left entirely on this plane. Oberon's championship of Hippolyta, "the bouncing Amazon, / [His] buskin'd mistress and [his] warrior love" (II.i.70–71), and Titania's of Theseus make a parallel necessary. We could, of course, argue that Oberon in wishing to take the Indian boy away from Titania is trying to show her how assinine her baby-love is, and is trying to have her emulate the more hunt-worthy vigorous pursuits of an Hippolyta. However, the Indian changeling boy bears too great similarity with the Idalian changeling boy, Ganymede, for us to be entirely satisfied with such an unerotic motive. Oberon's likeness to Jove further strengthens the possible Indian-Idalian relationship. Stealing away from fairyland and in "the shape of Corin" sitting all day piping love to a mortally "amorous Phillida" (II.i.65–68) recall Jove's escapades on one plane. Sporting with "the Morning's love . . . like a forester" (III.ii.389–90), which we tend to gloss over as if it were on a similar plane, that is, Jove dallying with Aurora, may figure Jove in quite another sphere of operation. The "Morning's love" may recall Aurora's love, Cephalus the hunter, and it is surely not a coincidence that Bottom-Pyramus declaring "love" to Flute-Thisby, kissing "the wall's hole" and not "lips at all" (V.i.204) suggests their love is truer than that between "Shafalus"-Cephalus and "Procrus"-Procris (V.i.201–2). And if we can understand Hero and Leander for Pyramus's "Limander" and Thisbe's "Helen" we cast further satiric light on the love relationship. Oberon-Jove's escapades suggest satiric levels for the play which May festivities (IV.i.137) in a green woods' context can quite conveniently carry.

Titania's championship of Theseus is motivated too, though she never quite realizes this. She exclaims "what visions [she] ha[s] seen" (IV.i.79) only in terms of dreading lest she had been "enamour'd of an ass" (IV.i.80) so that her reaction is equivalent to Bottom's description of his experience as "Bottom's Dream" (IV.i.220) which has no bottom to it. They by no means see themselves in the fierce vexation mirror, but imagine themselves "translated" (III.i.122).

Oberon accuses Titania of seducing Theseus away from the women he has ravished and with whom he has broken faith, with Perigouna, Aegles, Ariadne, and Antiopa. All Titania can do is suggest these are "the forgeries of jealousy" (II.i.81), but whether they are, her parallel crownings of the Indian boy and Bottom suggest that her "love to Theseus" (II.i.76) may not entirely be a figment. That she basically craves to be "the female ivy" (IV.i.46) desirous of the "barky fingers" (IV.i.47) of Bottom's "elm" (IV.i.47) is substantiated by the baby "lullaby" refrains to the fairies' song around "the cradle of the fairy queen" (III.i.80). Titania's love-lorn state is betrayed by her every move. When she and Oberon are "new in amity" (IV.i.91), it is because she has handed over the Indian boy. If this relationship is in any way a parallel for Theseus and Hippolyta it does not augur too well for a procreative marriage free from the "blots of Nature's hand . . . mole, harelip, . . . scar, / Nor mark prodigious" (V.i.416–19). Demetrius's remark, "are you sure / That we are [now] awake? It seems to me / That yet we sleep, we dream" (IV.i.196–98), is extraordinarily ironically pertinent to *all* the lovers' situations, because they have all been "practising behaviour to [their] own shadow" (*Twelfth Night* II.v.20–21) without being aware.

The fantasy world of *A Midsummer Night's Dream* is a vehicle for complete self-delusion, indeed for the utter sloughing of self with the potent force of real magic to furnish the necessary excuse for the victims. As in *Love's Labour's Lost* the bewitched characters are offered a glimpse of their own plight through the medium of a visual performance of the story of Pyramus and Thisbe, but they are too lost in the fascination of their dream effects to recognize themselves and their feelings. Nor are the immortals free from this delusion for Titania has her mirror of matronly concern for the Indian boy shattered when she is shown the stupidity of her action, and Oberon himself is shattered by the distorted effects of what he thought were quite simple methods of correction for his wife and for bemused mortals. Even the rude mechanicals aspire to play roles of grandeur in their translation. Lysander and Demetrius are as blind as Proteus and Valentine in the evaluation of their feelings and Hermia and Helena as interchangeable as Julia and Silvia in the game of pursuit and conquest. All are completely out of touch with reality and only Theseus apparently has sufficient awareness to question the validity of their hypnotic trance, but even he is not aware that it reveals his own unromantic conquest in such an unflattering light.

This is a world of shadows in which the glass has become clouded over by the breath of magic and the blurred image is mysteriously beautiful and much easier to live with than the truth.

THE EARLY TRAGEDIES

Titus Andronicus

If we may put on one side the vexed authorship question, and to do so is certainly fraught with great difficulties when even the champions of Shakespeare's authorship in the main are reluctant to dismiss the shades of Peele in particular, then it may be worthwhile examining *Titus* for any evidence of the shattered glass pattern, that is, for links in dramatic technique with the early comedies and histories.

The most startling observation, of course, must be that Titus in taking "false shadows for true substances" (III.ii.80) is by no means aware of the fact that his seeing has all along been at fault and still is, even in the grief wrought scene consequent on the mockery of his left-handed sacrifice sent back with the heads of his two sons, Martius and Quintus—later symbolized by the Clown's two pigeons in a basket. That his eyes "begin to dazzle" (III.ii. 85) he fobs off more as the excuse of age than of fault. That his right hand did not know what his left was doing and is thus as useless as the lopped off hand is ironically reinforced by his using only his mouth and his feet to guide the staff whereby he writes his name in sand—"in the dust [he] write[s] / [His] heart's deep languor and [his] soul's sad tears" (III.i.12–13). Like a clumsy animal he has nuzzled and stumbled and made his mark, has fallen into the "subtle hole . . . / Whose mouth is covered with" the "rude-growing briers" (II.iii.198–99) of his own unwitting planting. This is made abundantly clear by the course of his two sons, Martius and Quintus, who are literally brought to the "loathsome pit" (II.iii.176) by Aaron the "execrable wretch" (V.iii.177), the "black dog" (V.i.122), the perpetrator of "Acts of black night" (V.i.64), and plunged therein, but metaphorically have been cast there by their father's blindness.

Neither son is characterized for himself but is used dramatically as a shadow of the father. Their literal fall into "poor Bassianus' grave" (II.iii.240) parallels their father's falling into the metaphorical grave which he has dug for Bassianus, first by not championing his candidacy to the emperorship (possibly because he was trying publicly not to be seen as seeking power through Bassianus's betrothal to his daughter Lavinia), and secondly by giving his consent to Saturninus's request for his daughter Lavinia's hand in marriage when it is made perfectly obvious that Lavinia is Bassianus's lawfully betrothed. It is easy to see why Saturninus makes this move in an attempt to strengthen his position; it brilliantly circumvents Titus. Titus, like Theseus, might try to excuse his ignorance of the betrothal by pleading that "being over-full of self-affairs, / [His] mind did lose" (*Dream* I.i.113–14) knowledge of it, but the actions of Lavinia's brothers in support of Bassianus's prior claim on her, one of them, Mutius, going so far as to give his life at Titus's hands defending it, belie him.

Titus's blind killing of his son is destroying the very staff he is trying to lean on. All his railing about Mutius and refusing to allow him to be buried in the family vault because he has not died in his country's honor is a grim comment on his blindness, and a forecast of his own ignominious death.

That the fall of Martius and Quintus into the "fell devouring receptacle" (II.iii.235) should be likened to Pyramus's disaster, as he "by night lay bath'd in maiden blood" (II.iii.232), is most ironically appropriate. The "fierce vexation of [the] dreame" of the house of Titus that it can restore to Saturninus, the late emperor's elder son, the "people's hearts and wean them from themselves" (I.i.211) and create an emperor of him "whose virtues will" it is hoped "Reflect on Rome as [Titan's] rays on earth, / And ripen justice in this commonweal" (I.i.225–27), is soon shattered. Titus cannot wean his own heart entirely from the emperorship. Somewhat Coriolanus fashion he hastens not to have his "nothings monster'd" (*Coriolanus* II.ii.81), and pleads only for a staff of honor for his age not a sceptre "to control the world" (I.i.199) when his brother Marcus and the tribunes name him "in election for the empire" (I.i.183), but in his over forceful championship of Saturninus he is, Warwick-like, making the King and acting as his shadow.

His basic reason for standing out against Bassianus's prior claim on Lavinia in favor of granting Saturninus's request that she be made "Rome's royal mistress, mistress of [Saturninus's] heart" (I.i.241) is that through Lavinia publicly requested as empress he holds himself highly honored and can consecrate his sword, chariot, and prisoners—offerings "well worthy Rome's imperious lord" (I.i.250), because he is emperor in all but name. But his very offerings are his downfall, for in his introduction of Tamora, Queen of the Goths, he is Sinon fashion (like Margaret in *2 Henry VI* and Richard in *Richard III*) bringing "the fatal engine in" (V.iii.86) that begins that "baleful burning night" (V.iii.83) of his own Troy's destruction.

By allowing his sons unnecessarily to butcher Alarbus,

61

Tamora's oldest son, ostensibly for the purpose of "appeas[ing] [the] groaning shadows" (I.i.126) of those of his own sons killed in honorable wars with the Goths, he is trying to appease the groaning shadow of his own ambitions, and moreover, is creating a dreadful ironic precedent. Killing Alarbus in cold blood as a religious sacrifice parallels killing Mutius in cold blood as a sacrifice to his own "irreligious piety" |I.i.130), and is basically self-immolation. Refusing to have Mutius buried in the family tomb "sumptuously re-edified" (I.i.351) by himself, where "none but soldiers and Rome's servitors" (I.i.352) are buried, is a self indictment, because it was at his own hand that his son was "basely slain" (I.i.353) in a brawl. What irony it is, too, that the very sons who religiously asked Titus for the sacrifice of Alarbus for their slain brethren religiously ask Titus for the burial of Mutius "with [their] brethren" (I.i.348). Nothing can appease Titus's groaning shadow, nothing will give his "fearful slumber" (III.i.253) an end, nothing will save him from the accusation by both parties of being "barbarous" (I.i.131,378), till he be eased with being nothing.

By killing his son Mutius for defending Bassianus's abduction of his betrothed Lavinia he is giving further strength to the butchery pattern and unconsciously allying himself with his enemies' destructive intentions for himself. When he gives in to his sons' and brother's supplications and allows Mutius to be buried in the family tomb—"Well, bury him, and bury me the next" (I.i.386) he little realises just how much truth there is in the random remark.

The very sight of Tamora as she is handed over by Titus to Saturninus is the undoing of any influence Titus might have had over Saturninus, despite the latter's last words before "seeing" Tamora that Titus is the "father of [his] life" (I.i.253), and his injunction to the Romans to forget their loyalty to himself when he forgets the least of Titus's "unspeakable deserts" (I.i.256). Edward IV's and Henry VI's leanings on Warwick are convenient parallels.

That Titus should think Tamora is beholding to him that "brought her for this high good turn so far" (I.i.397) is much more a measure of Lucius's remark about him, "He is not with himself" (I.i.368), than it is of the remark in its context of Titus's refusal to bury Mutius. Titus cannot give up metaphorical emperorship. He made himself the shadow of an emperor but insists on being treated as if he were the real substance. He not only made Saturnine emperor but made Tamora empress also. The rapidity with which he can shift his stand from Lavinia's potential empressship to Tamora's fait accompli indicates well enough that it is his own power through them that matters and not the strength of their individual claims. The rapidity with which Saturninus allows himself to be captivated by Tamora is best understood as the result of his subconscious determination not to be thought of as having "begg'd the empire at [Titus's] hands" (I.i.307). By making Tamora his own and not just Titus's gift he is trying to lay the ghost of power which he feels shadows him.

Hoping to sway through Tamora, that is, taking the false shadow of Tamora for the real substance, Titus is an easy victim to the all too substantive flattery of Tamora's daring to undertake on her honor "For good Lord Titus' innocence in all" (I.i.437), and quite unaware of the shadowy Alarbus revenge theme which will raze the "cruel father and his traitorous sons" (I.i.452). The flattery of the empress's prevailing on Saturninus "infuse[s] new life" (I.i.461) in Titus, according to his own verdict, but the kiss of peace is the Judas kiss of a Richard III. The new found amity is to be celebrated at Titus's suggestion by the hunting of the panther and the hart, little aware as he is that the panther is to be Bassianus and the hart Lavinia, and that in the panther's pit he will lose two of his sons and lose himself in grief over their deaths.

The hunt of Act II, rich in the subtle mingling of the Ovidian imagery and language of Venus and Adonis, Diana and Actaeon and Philomel and Tereus, continues the carefully organized symmetry of Act I. What ironic justice it is that Tamora must also take false shadows for real substances—she is a shadowy empress to Saturnine but a substantive slave to Aaron, whose letter and word of promise she carries so intimately. The situation somewhat resembles Queen Margaret's in *1* and *2 Henry VI* in which Margaret is Suffolk's mistress, minus the complications of the particular "joyless, dismal, black, and sorrowful issue" (IV.ii.66).

When Bassianus and Lavinia surprise Tamora in her rencontre with Aaron they see the substance of a charge against her being conducted by her foul desire to wander to an obscure plot accompanied "but with a barbarous Moor" (II.iii.78), refer openly to Tamora's leaving her "snow-white goodly steed" to enjoy her "raven-coloured love" (II.iii.76,83), but by no means realise that the black and white that are being caught are themselves—the panther and the "dainty doe" (II.ii.26).

Titus salutes the morning of the hunt with a panegyric on nature—"the morn is bright and grey, / The fields are fragrant and the woods are green" (II.ii.1–2) in very similar terms to Tamora's claim that everything "doth make a gleeful boast" . . . "The birds chant melody on every bush, / The snake lies rolled in the cheerful sun, / The green leaves quiver with the cooling wind" (II.iii.11–14)—a "nurse's song / Of lullaby to bring her babe asleep" (II.iii.28–29) (strangely similar imagery to Titania's boudoir lullaby), but the day's soft shadows ("a chequer'd shadow on the ground"—"sweet shade" [II.iii.15,16]) are overcast by Titus's having been "troubled in [his] sleep this night" (II.ii.9) and by Tamora's being thwarted of a Dido and Aeneas "happy storm" (II.iii.23) affaire d'amour by the intrusion of Bassianus and Lavinia. The "gleeful boast" of Tamora's description of nature which she makes before the interruption, is immediately turned to a vengeance call to her newly arrived sons, Chiron and Demetrius, on Bassianus and Lavinia for calling her a "foul adulteress" (II.iii.109) in the "barren detested vale" (II.iii.93) of the "abhorred pit" (II.iii.98). The snakes cheerfully rolling in the sun now become a "thousand fiends, a thousand hissing snakes" (II.iii.100) where "never shines the sun" (II.iii.96). The hunt becomes a descent into the "Cimmerian" (II.iii.72) land of shadows where "nothing breeds" (II.iii.96) except the harbingers of death—"the nightly owl or fatal raven" (II.iii.97), and the pit which receives first Bassianus's "dead trunk" (II.iii.130) and then Martius's and Quintus's all too living bodies becomes "Cocytus' misty mouth" (II.iii.236).

Lavinia's fate is to wander through a living grave of the fields of mourning, "deflow'red" (II.iv.26), "lopp'd and hew'd" (II.iv.17) and her tongue cut out by worse than devils, for if but Tereus had "heard the heavenly harmony / Which that sweet tongue hath made, / He would have dropp'd his knife" (II.iv.48–50) and fallen asleep as the three-headed guardian of the gates of Hades did on hearing Orpheus. Those arms "Whose circling shadows kings ha[d] sought to sleep in" (II.iv.19) have been lopped off by the Cimmerian shadows of the king. Her tongue which pleaded to Tamora to keep her from Chiron and Demetrius's "worse than killing lust" (II.iii.175) by killing her herself and tumbling her body "into some loathsome pit" (II.iii.176) has but too eloquently "stood upon her chastity" (II.iii.124), and berated Tamora's "goodly gift in horning" (II.iii.67) and must be cut out by the "bastard-ized" Chiron and Demetrius, who are soon faced with their "brother"—Aaron's "first-born son and heir!" (IV.ii.92). Her chastity, the loyalty of her nuptial vow, the "nice-preserved honesty" (II.iii.135), the "painted hope" that "braves [Tamora's] mightiness" (II.iii.126) must be destroyed by the "tiger's young ones" (II.iii.142) "wrapt in [their mother's] hide" (*3 Henry VI* I.iv. 137). What irony it is that Lavinia tries to put her hope in "every mother breeds not sons alike" (II.iii.146) and that though "the raven doth not hatch a lark" (II.iii.149) it is thought by some that "ravens foster forlorn children / The whilst their own birds famish in their nests" (II.iii.153–54). Titus greets Aaron's news that a lopped off hand from any one of the remaining Andronici (Titus, Marcus, Lucius) will ransom both his sons, Martius and Quintus, "for their fault" (III.i.156) with joy that "ever raven s[a]ng so like a lark" (III.i.158), and even Aaron conceives the plan of substituting the *fair* child of one of his countrymen in the place of his own "thick-lipp'd" (IV.ii.175) offspring in the hope that a false shadow shall be mistaken for a true substance.

And yet it is not with Lavinia's lost innocence, elo-quence, and power to circle kings within the shadow of her arms that we are primarily concerned. Lavinia is only Titus's tool (just as his sons Martius and Quintus are), as her death at his hands and as her parallel situation, writing names in dust by means of staff guided by mouth and feet only, make perfectly clear. Through her is mirrored the destruction of Titus's own power to circle kings within the shadow of his mighty arms: through her is shattered the image of the innocence with which he could cry "Rome and the righteous heavens be my judge, / How I have lov'd

and honoured Saturnine!" (I.i.426–27), the innocence for
which Tamora vouched: through her are refracted the rays
of his eloquence which fail to reach the ears of the judges,
senators, and tribunes. When Marcus finds Lavinia like a
stricken deer seeking to hide herself it is an image of Titus
himself who envies the fact that his son Lucius has been
banished for attempting to rescue his two brothers from
their death. But Marcus is blind in thinking that the sight
of Lavinia will "make [her] father blind" (II.iv.52). Titus
has reprimanded Lucius for being blind in moaning about
his "everlasting doom of banishment" (III.i.51), when
Rome that is but a "wilderness of tigers" (III.i.54) by
banishing him has befriended him (almost in Kent's terms
and Coriolanus's terms), but Titus does not see how he
himself has played the tiger, how he himself has been the
fool that "added water to the sea" (III.i.68) and "brought
a faggot to bright-burning Troy" (III.i.69), and unlike
Lear he never does see, or even begin to see. Ironically, he
now waxes poetically eloquent not on his wisdom but on
his blindness. A man of grief overwhelmed by each surge of
incoming waves he is not a man "More sinn'd against than
sinning" (*Lear* III.ii.60) but entirely sinned against and
unaware of sinning in any respect.

When he exclaims that if he had but seen the "picture"
of Lavinia in this plight it would have madded him, and
does not know what to do now he beholds her "lively body
so" (III.i.105) he is ironically showing he lives and walks
with shadows not with substances. Suggesting that they all
look into a clear fountain and gaze so long that the fountain be made a "brine-pit with [their] bitter tears"
(III.i.129) is a bitter self-indictment. Titus is not looking
into the clear waters of the fountain to see himself but
ironically to make it impossible to *see* anything. The situation parallels Richard II looking into the misty glass of his

tears, but Richard, however momentarily, does see himself a traitor with the rest. Titus is still in Richard's attitudinizing stages, wanting to weep the fountains salty, "Plot some device of further misery" (III.i.134) and "tell sad stories of the death of kings" (*Richard II* III.ii.156)— "chanced in the times of old" (III.ii.83). The greatest irony of all, however, is his suggestion that Marcus, Lucius, and himself cut away their hands and bite out their tongues "and in dumb shows / Pass the remainder of [their] hateful days" (III.i.131–32). He wants to make himself a king of snow, like Richard II, dripping into the fountain of his own grief, or a molehill king like Henry VI in a "sympathy of woe" (III.i.148) entirely unaware that it was himself who set the hunting of the panther and the doe going, who created the foul pit.

Aaron coming in with the news that a lopped hand will save the heads of Martius and Quintus points the irony still further. Titus already caught in shadowy attitudinizing cannot now see that what looks like the real substance, the real cutting off of his hand, is only a mockery of his woe. How dramatically appropriate it is that while Marcus and Lucius go off to fetch an axe still haggling about which of them shall provide the hand Titus asks Aaron to lend him his hand, and he will give him his (III.i.188). In league with this thing of darkness, which he does not know or ever will know how to acknowledge as his, he deceives Marcus and Lucius, but most of all himself. He has now bereft himself of the only power he had left. With his instructions to Aaron to bid the emperor bury the hand "that warded him / From thousand dangers" (III.i.195– 96) he is ironically burying the last vestige of his military power, though by cutting off the *left* hand he imagines he still has the *right* for power.

When a little later Lavinia is bidden to bear his hand

between her teeth (III.i.283) the total ruined image of Titus in so far as Lavinia can reflect it is completed. His slaying of her at the end of the play becomes thus symbolic of his own suicide. Lavinia represents one part of the image which his own hand shattered.

Titus is immediately buried, too, in "bottomless" (III.i.218) woes and miseries, giving vent to "deep extremes" (III.i.216), like Lear in the storm, but again without the notion of "sinning" as well as being sinned against, or like Richard refusing to be comforted by Carlisle and Aumerle. When the hand is returned with the two heads it was supposed to have saved Titus refuses to let sorrow "usurp upon [his] wat'ry eyes / And make them blind with tributary tears" (III.i.269–70), but proceeds to be blinded by Revenge, not the practical revenge policy of his son Lucius, who will go "to the Goths, and raise a pow'r" (III.i.300), but the self-annihilating revenge, because he vows to return the mischiefs again "Even in their throats that [have] committed them" (III.i.275), and this must, of course, destroy himself, though he little realises.

Face to face with his "map of woe" (III.ii.12), Lavinia, he tries to show it how to wound its heart with sighing, kill it with groans or with a little knife between its teeth make a little hole through which to drown its heart with tears. It represents for him a repetition of the tale "How Troy was burnt and [Aeneas] made miserable" (III.ii.28), in which he identifies himself with Aeneas, instead of with Sinon. He claims he can interpret all the "map of woe['s]" "martyr'd signs" (III.ii.36) and will wrest an alphabet from all its marks and practise to know its meaning, but the imagery is empty of self-revelation: it is another means of revelling in his misery.

He chides Marcus for killing a fly, a "deed of death done

on the innocent" (III.ii.56) unbecoming of Titus's brother,
and says that the action has killed his heart, when in point
of fact his own killing of Alarbus and Mutius was far more
irresponsible and disastrous. When Marcus suggests the fly
was "black ill-favour'd" and like "to the Empress' Moor"
(III.ii.66–67) the deed is commended by Titus, for it is
the very line for his own revenge. Thus the killing of the
fly, Tamora, is in many ways a prefiguring of himself, and
it is dramatically appropriate that in killing Tamora himself he should accuse her of literally "Eating the flesh that
she herself hath bred" (V.iii.62), when in point of fact the
charge is all but literally true of himself. He mistakes the
shadow of Tamora for the true substance of himself.

Titus is quick to assist Lavinia in writing the names of
her ravagers in the sand and to plead that heaven guide her
pen to "print [her] sorrows plain" (IV.i.75) that the
traitors and the truth may be known, but only in the spirit
of "discover[ing] for revenge" (IV.i.74), that the hunt may
be engaged on and the quarry hounded to its death, but by
the subtlest means lest the victims have wind of his intent.
Hamlet fashion he wants the satisfaction of annoying his
enemies, Chiron and Demetrius, by sending them "weapons
wrapp'd about with lines / That wound, beyond their feeling, to the quick" (IV.ii.27–28). Chiron and Demetrius are
certainly incapable of appreciating their significance, but
Aaron is perceptive and notes that "were our witty empress
well afoot, / She would applaud Andronicus' conceit"
(IV.ii.29–30). Again Titus is mistaking the shadow for the
true substance.

His railing on justice, *Terras Astraea reliquit* (IV.iii.4),
resembles Lear's only in its gusto, lacking any suggestion,
however, that the railer even partially identifies himself
with handy-dandy justice, for Titus is "wrung with wrongs
more than [his] back[] can bear" (IV.iii.48). He thunders

70

with Mars and Jove, lightens with Apollo and Mercury, does not so much "solicit heaven and move the gods / To send down Justice for to wreak [his] wrongs" (IV.iii.50–51) as Tamburlaine-wise to usurp the role of the gods, trying psychologically to compensate for his earlier expression of weakness—"we are but shrubs, no cedars we, / No big-bon'd men fram'd of the Cyclops' size" (IV.iii.45–46)—trying to give greater substance to his shadow. But the immense power falls short of its target in its shooting "off one of Taurus' horns" (IV.iii.69) and landing (Pallus > Phallus? fashion) in *un*-Virgo's lap with the cuckolding "Empress' villain" (IV.iii.73).

And the entry of the Clown with two pigeons in his basket, whom Titus ironically misidentifies with Jupiter's "carrier" and petulantly cannot understand why he has not "come from heaven" (IV.iii.88), reduces the wronged Titus figure still further. The two pigeons, symbols of his two sons whom he has unwittingly slain, are a fitting offering to be sent to the Court by a Clown with a supplication on Titus's behalf. The Clown was going with his pigeons "to the tribunal plebs, to take up a matter of / brawl betwixt [his] uncle and one of the emperal's / men" (IV.iii.92–94): as ambassador of Titus he reduces Titus's wrongs to a "matter of brawl." The shade of Mutius, who was "basely slain in brawls" (I.i.353) by his father hangs about the embassade. The play is turning back on these incidents: things are rounding out. The "shade" of Tamora encounters with him in the name of that very Revenge he had sought hell in vain for. He had threatened to "dive into the burning lake below" (IV.iii.43) and pull "Revenge from hell" (IV.iii.38), but Revenge chooses to confound his plots.

Face to face with Tamora (Revenge) and her sons Chiron and Demetrius (Rapine and Murder) he craftily

71

pretends that his "miserable, mad, mistaking eyes" (V.ii.66) see the Empress and the Empress's sons, knowing them all the time and allowing them to suppose him mad so that he may "o'erreach them in their own devices" (V.ii.143). What is far more important, however, is that he does not recognize that this Revenge figure talking to him of the "hollow cave or lurking-place" (V.ii.35), this "vast obscurity or misty vale" (V.ii.36), where murder and death are perpetrated, is the shadow of himself. "O, had [he] never, never hunted there!" (IV.i.56).

Lavinia, deflowered, lopped, and holding her father's lopped left hand in her teeth is one part of the shattered image of Titus: Tamora (Revenge) with Chiron and Demetrius (Rapine and Murder) at her side (Proserpine and her "two proper palfreys, black as jet" (V.ii.50)—"A pair of cursed hell-hounds and their dam") (V.ii.144) are another! What "mad, mistaking eyes"—"What [tragic] error drives [his] eyes and ears amiss" (*Comedy of Errors* II.ii.186).

Demetrius and Chiron ask Titus to show them a murderer and "a villain that hath done a rape" (V.ii.94) and they will be "reveng'd on him" (V.ii.95), and Titus's crafty answer, "when thou find'st a man that's like thyself" (V.ii.99) he is a murderer, he is a ravisher, is powerfully ironic in its non-recognition of self. He has "lesson'd" (V.ii.110) Tamora and her sons, but has not taken the heart of the lesson to himself. With the guilty blood of Chiron and Demetrius and their ground down bones he can make a piecrust and have Tamora eat her guilt in the fantastic wedding feast of the Centaurs: Tamora shall be physically wedded to her evil deeds. Titus is projecting his guilt on her, though he would never "see" to acknowledge it. That is why Tamora's death and Titus's are practically in the same instant of time with Lavinia's—"eating the flesh that [he] himself hath bred" (V.iii.62).

But the play significantly does not end with the triple death. That the remaining Andronici should project all the family's guilt on to Aaron, the "execrable wretch / That hath been breeder of these dire events" (V.ini.177–78) is another instance of how "worldly men" with their "mad, mistaking eyes" exonorate themselves at an obvious criminal's expense.

Titus hardly deserves to be buried in the Andronici's "household monument" (V.iii.194) for his past victory over the Goths any more than Tamora deserves any "funeral rite" or "mournful bell shall ring her burial" (V.iii.196–97). That part of him which colleagued with the shade of Tamora ought to be thrown "forth to beasts and birds to prey" (V.iii.198); that part of him which colleagued with the shade of Aaron ought to be set "breast-deep in earth" (V.iii.179) and allowed to famish: that part of him which set the hunt for the panther and the doe going ought not to find its resting place in the tomb of the Andronici, but in the panther's pit, but that part of him which wished however blindly to do the right things and unwittingly did the wrong allows him honorable burial as far as Lucius and Marcus wish to interpret it.

Aaron, who is made almost a chorus at the end with his long speeches of "wondrous things"—"murders, rapes, and massacres, / Acts of black night, abominable deeds, / Complots of mischief, treason, villainies" (V.i.63–65), who confesses to a "thousand more" deeds than the play gives warrant of (V.i.125–44), each one of which he would have willingly done "as one would kill a fly," and only repents that he "cannot do ten thousand more" (V.i.144), cannot sensibly be used as *the* villain of the play. He is the black shadow to everyone else's substantive evil. He has no moral code, nor pretends to have, except to believe in the force of morality on others, Lucius in particular. This is the force of his remarks to Lucius, whom he knows to be "religious" and to have "a thing within [him] called conscience" (V.i.74–75). He tries to draw himself apart and almost breaks his heart with extremely malevolent-puckish laughter, prying through the crevice of a wall at Titus, and monstrously delighting in the foolishness of Titus. And yet the irony of it all is that he may well think he is the *real* substance of the tragedy, that every evil perpetrated has stemmed from him. Here is the significance of his inability to hush his child's crying which gives him away. His subconscious cries out for recognition. He *needs* to be acclaimed as the master villain and loses no opportunity to draw such attention to himself.

There is, however, no doubt that in Aaron's concern for the child he is betraying something that is not so shadowy. Titus's children were made pawns to his family honor: Aaron's child, of royal blood, is tangible evidence of his father's all too *human* success.

When comedy is the medium of presentation the refusal to face one's image in the glass may seem a little sad, even regrettable, and indeed some of the victims of this self-delusion do not escape totally unscathed, but the consequences lack the magnitude and significance of the same phenomenon on the tragic level. Titus's tragedy is that he can turn a blind eye on his own weaknesses and so easily persuade himself that his lust for power, his craving for recognition, are in reality the pursuit of noble honor and high ideals. To gain his selfish ends Titus does not hesitate to use and sacrifice those whom he professes to hold dear. Titus looks into the glass and sees not himself and his own failings but the imagined wrongs of everyone else for which he must seek revenge. The blindness of Titus has a malevolent quality which humiliates and destroys everyone in his path and finally strips Titus himself of every vestige of the

74

honor he sought with such fiendish singlemindedness. Titus shatters the glass rather than face the image of himself without power and glory, and in doing so shatters his whole life and the lives of those closest to him leaving the fragments for the despised Aaron to gloat over and take undue credit for.

King John

With John there is not so much an inability to see himself as there is a deliberate refusal to see the necessity for such introspection when none can really call his power to account, and power, exercised in one form or another, is sufficient in and by itself. It is as if we were faced with the kind of king Richard II might have been had he discovered his lion strength *before* the thought of a Bolingbroke could be allowed to materialize. John is determined to keep his throne by *strong possession,* by sheer physical and mental efforts, and it is because no stronger dramatis persona than himself emerges as his enemy that he is successful in doubly keeping his throne for himself and handing it over at his death to his son Prince Henry. John really is more akin to Bolingbroke than Richard II in this and in many other respects, but because he is not challenged by another self, a Hotspur—"even as [he] was then is Percy now" (*1 Henry IV* III.ii.96), he is not obliged to tackle himself and can remain "Exterior form, outward accoutrement" (I.i.211) with no necessity to penetrate his glass in "inward motion" (I.i.212). He successfully keeps himself to himself, not even allowing the audience to triumph with "O, now you look like [John]! all this while / You were disguis'd" (IV.i.126–27), except possibly for the abortive pangs of conscience on the believed execution of his plans for Arthur's death.

That there was good dramatic potential for such introspection should the course of unfolding events call it forth
is made abundantly clear in the very beginning of the play.
John knows he is a usurper. His mother, Queen Eleanor,
represents the whispering of conscience in his ear that
"strong possession much more than [his] right" (I.i.40) is
his best line of approach. He allows her to carry the burden
of his conscience for him so that it does not worry him, and
to give voluble expression to his forceful hold on the
throne. She continues to represent John's political acumen,
awareness of his enemies' moves, and military might in
France (I.i.150; III.ii.80) until her death, at which time
John recognizes "How wildly then walks [his] estate in
France!" (IV.ii.128) without his "mother's care" (IV.ii.
117), until he finds a substitute in the Bastard.

It is not accidental that on both occasions when John
allows himself to exclaim on his mother's death—"What!
mother dead!" (IV.ii.127) ; "My mother dead!" (IV.ii.181),
he is greeted by adverse prophecies which relate to his
losing somehow the "circle of [his] glory" (V.i.2) which
strong possession had temporarily maintained as his. The
death of his mother is used dramatically to throw the
weight of conscience, however momentarily, back to him,
though he shrugs it off as best he can.

Peter of Pomfret's prophecy that before noon on next
Ascension day John will yield up his crown, and Hubert's
news of the five moons—"Four fixed, and the fifth did
whirl about / The other four in wondrous motion" (IV.ii.
183–84) dramatically reveal John's losing grip on the
throne. The first is explicit. John, in imprisoning Peter to
be hanged on the day of the prophecy's supposed fulfilment, first tries to deliver himself safely from the "idle
dreamer['s]" (IV.ii.153) prognostication by this act of
strong possession, and then afterwards subconsciously

equivocates by yielding up his crown voluntarily to the papal legate—"I did suppose it should be on constraint; / But, heaven be thank'd, it is but voluntary" (V.i.28–29)— thus trying to take the prophecy's sting away.

John's handling of Peter's prophecy is typical of his whole approach throughout the play. By strong physical or mental possession the power of his enemies shall dwindle, and if he can keep active this way there is no need to think of conscience.

The second augury, unlike that of the three suns in *2 Henry VI* with which it invites immediate parallel, is *deliberately* veiled for dramatic purposes. John cannot equivocate with it, cannot physically or mentally grasp its implications, but can only fear. And the form the fear takes is a determined projection of his guilt over the believed death of Arthur (the true claimant to the throne, the son of John's elder brother, Geoffrey) on Hubert, the agent of the murder, whom he himself seduced to do the deed. The situation parallels somewhat Bolingbroke's. Bolingbroke may exclaim against Exton, the murderer of Richard II, "Though I did wish him dead, / I hate the murderer, love him murdered" (*Richard II* V.vi.39–40), and try to give Exton the "guilt of conscience" for his labor, but have to go on a mental pilgrimage of atonement himself for the rest of his life: John's "I had a mighty cause / To wish him dead, but thou hadst none to kill him" (IV.ii.205–6) followed by the consideration that "when the last accompt 'twixt heaven and earth / Is to be made, then shall this hand and seal / Witness against us to damnation" (IV.ii.216–18) apparently leads him to genuine pangs of conscience. Lessening his own guilt at the expense of Hubert as much as he can, he nevertheless does come to suggest, Brutus and Lear fashion, that "his little world of man" (*Lear* III.i.10) "Like to a little kingdom, suffers then / The nature of an insurrection" (*Julius Caesar* II.i.68–69), for "Hostility and civil tumult reigns / Between [his] conscience and [his] cousin's death" (IV.ii.247–48), and if Hubert were not in a position to "make a peace between [his] soul and [him]" (IV.ii.250) by revealing that Arthur is alive there might well have been a shattering of John's glass, but the turn of events makes it entirely unnecessary. It is as if Hubert stood for the equivocation of John's conscience until sheer opportunism like sheer commodity resolves the dilemma to leave him still in possession.

News of Arthur's being alive is not greeted by John as a means of making peace between his tortured conscience and himself but as a means of making peace between his revolted lords and himself, thereby reinforcing his previous position. And from then on there is a complete return to possession by subtle force. John is caught up in a whirl of activity with which he is physically no longer able to cope, hence the appropriateness of granting the Bastard "the ordering of this present time" (V.i.77). The fever "that hath troubled [him] so long" (V.iii.3) and that lies heavy on his sick heart is spoken of predominantly in literal terms. The "tyrant fever" (V.iii.14) of the poison which burns him up and which ironically will not be assuaged by any of his kingdom's commodities becomes on John's final admission a hellish "fiend confin'd to tyrannize / On unreprievable condemned blood" (V.vii.47–48). This is not Lear's "wheel of fire" by any means. The revelation that finally closes his earthly suffering is not self revelation but the fact that the best part of his royal power was "in the Washes all unwarily / Devoured by the unexpected flood" (V.vii.63–64).

It is ironically appropriate that John should expire when the *means* for strong possession are suddenly no longer there, and it is ironically appropriate that the child Prince Henry, John's son, should unite in fealty all his subjects in a strong image of England "Now these her princes are come home again" (V.vii.115). It is as if the four claims to the English throne, John's and Salisbury's as surviving sons of Henry II, Arthur's as surviving son of Geoffrey deceased son of Henry II, and Lewis's through his marriage with Blanche, niece to King John, had all been struck by the new moon of Prince Henry, the lineal state and glory of the land.

The claims of Arthur and then Lewis provide the play's structural dimensions, and it is painfully easy to write them off as disorganized elements, but each in turn derives its importance from the extent to which it provides valuable dramatic comment on John's.

Arthur's claim is entirely legitimate: John's illegitimate. John has "under-wrought his lawful king" and "done a rape / Upon the maiden virtue of the crown" (II.i.97–98). The whole situation is beautifully paralleled by his championship of the Bastard over Robert Faulconbridge, the legitimate son and heir of old Sir Robert Faulconbridge. The irony of John's asking the Bastard why the younger brother lays claim to his inheritance and being told he knows no reason "except to get the land" (I.i.73) is acute. The situation is even more intense when John dismisses the illegitimacy of the Bastard—"Your brother is legitimate. / Your father's wife did after wedlock bear him" (I.i.116–17). John, subconsciously fighting the parallel between himself and the younger brother, is trying desperately to have that elder brother's claim perfectly legitimized and honorable. On a point of law he is right in claiming that since the Bastard was born *after* Sir Robert Faulconbridge's return from overseas he cannot therefore be bastardized, because no child born of a married woman could be thus stigmatized unless the husband was beyond the four seas during the whole period of the wife's pregnancy. But only on a point of *law*. In point of *fact* the Bastard revels in his bastardy, and both John and Queen Eleanor are rushed off their feet by the recognition that the Bastard's father was indeed Richard I. Both of them welcome this slip of Richard I's with open arms, thus signifying their acceptance of his position and their own bastardizing.

When John knights the Bastard as Sir Richard Plantagenet after he has agreed to follow the fortunes of the Plantagenets and bequeath his lands to his younger brother, the kingly position is brilliantly exposed. The younger Faulconbridge has been made a "landed squire" not only by the "landless knight" of his elder brother, Philip the Bastard, but also and much more significantly so by the "landless knight" of King John, "John Lackland." The elder Faulconbridge has been accepted as a natural son of Richard I and knighted as Sir Richard, paying obeisance to John. By this equivocal means John has absorbed in himself a claim to the throne which is more directly in line than Arthur's. It is important to recognize this clearly. Philip the Bastard, now knighted Sir Richard Plantagenet, as son of Richard I supersedes Arthur, son of Geoffrey. He never pushes his own claim, however, even though he is concerned with the "footsteps of [his] rising" (I.i.216), serves John faithfully, and leads the way in bequeathing his "faithful services / And true subjection everlastingly" (V.vii.104–5) to Prince Henry, on John's death. He does not really exist dramatically for his own sake so much as for a projection of John's zestful illegitimate vigor.

By absorbing Philip the Bastard's complete loyalty John has also invigorated his "strong possession" of the throne.

The spirit of Richard I—"the very spirit of Plantagenet" (I.i.167), has been captured in Faulconbridge and allied in John's cause rather than allowed to stalk his usurpation of Prince Arthur's rights. Arthur's acceptance of the service of the Archduke of Austria in the name of retribution for Austria's part in "Coeur-de-lion's death" (II.i.12) weakly parallels this. Austria may exclaim that he will return no more to his home until England salutes Arthur for her king, may *talk* about a "just and charitable war" (II.i.36), but his weakness is not far to seek, and one of the play's most poignant ironies is that Philip the Bastard, picking up the cue from Constance, Arthur's mother, repeatedly calls Austria's bluff by threatening to "hang a calf's-skin on those recreant limbs" (III.i.131,133,199,220,299), and successfully proves his point by killing him in battle. The spirit of Coeur-de-lion has indeed been avenged in a much more satisfying way; not by a weak nephew who has to be "shadow[ed]" (II.i.14) under Austria's wings, but by a vigorous natural son.

The first great scene in the play sets the seal on John's method of procedure. Recognizing that compromise and equivocation take the sting out of charges against him John carefully and brilliantly devitalizes his enemies' power. He not only "lays you plots" (III.iv.146) as the papal legate points out, but the weaknesses of his enemies and the times conspire with him.

This explains, too, why Hubert manages to win his way to the very heart of John's attachment from being merely chief citizen of the beseiged Angiers, which is bold in its determination to give allegiance only to him "that proves the King" (II.i.270). He is taken into the bosom of John's counsel because he found a way to keep Angiers in strong possession, and this against the united opposition of both John's and Arthur's parties. In the battle for Angiers, symbolically the battle for title of King of England and her French possessions, John first tried sheer force and claimed, as it turned out, as doubtful a victory as his enemies—"Strength match'd with strength, and power confronted power. / Both are alike" (II.i.330–31). The Bastard's plan for the opposing parties to unite in razing Angiers and *then* fighting over its possession is in line with John's thinking, especially in the design to have his enemies Austria and France in their imprudent discipline to rain their bullets on Angiers, Austria from the north, France from the south "in each other's mouth" (II.i.414), but Hubert's plan to marry the Dauphin to Blanche, King John's niece, is closer, as the Bastard is quick to recognize —"not a word of his / But buffets better than a fist of France" (II.i.464–65).

Queen Eleanor's whispering in his ear that by this marriage he will "surely tie [His] now unsur'd assurance to the crown" (II.i.470–71) is but his political answer to his conscience. Hubert's plan assures John's strong possession because it rains metaphorical bullets between Arthur's camp and the French and Austrian camps that have now colleagued with Arthur's enemy. It is significant that for the time being John retains Angiers alone of all his French provinces for himself. Symbolically it now stands for his conquest and maintainance of his title, and for his victory over French and Austrian support of Arthur, but he knows how to use this as a tool to help "heal up all" (II.i.550) when the need arises.

The Dauphin is taking Blanche, in accepting Hubert's and John's terms, becomes not only a shadow of Blanche, and through her of John, but a shadow of himself, losing the very substance of his honor, armed in Arthur's rights. The Bastard is quick to draw the inference that the Dauphin "doth espy / Himself love's traitor" (II.i.506–7).

He is also the shadow of his father, King Philip, who is uneasy in his conscience about reneging on Arthur's rights. The crowning irony of all is that John makes peace between their consciences and themselves by creating Arthur "Duke of Bretagne / And Earl of Richmond" (II.i.551–52), and by appointing him lord of Angiers. This last is symbolically the only way in which John will give Arthur back his kingship. By this means John has absorbed Arthur's rights within himself in so far as the French and Austrians are concerned. By trading in "commodity," "this vile drawing bias, / This sway of motion" (II.i.577–78), which has drawn France and Austria from a "resolv'd and honourable war" (II.i.585) John has once again asserted "strong possession" more than his right, and has fobbed off his enemies with nothing more than a metaphorical philosopher's stone. King Philip's remarks on the wedding of Blanche and Lewis that the glorious sun solemnizes the day by playing "the alchemist, / Turning with splendour of his precious eye / The meagre cloddy earth to glittering gold" (III.i.78–80) show just how far folly has usurped his mind. Arthur's real golden rights to the throne have been exchanged for the flimsy gold of their "own vantage['s]" (II.i.550) commodity. John has done an Autolycus on them picking their pockets of their real worth and substituting baubles.

Arthur's own progress follows a similar pattern. Taken by sheer force in battle, handed over by John to a forceful plan for his extinction, he survives by the all too effective use of his eloquent innocence. The scene is a much more powerful version of the death of Rutland in 2 *Henry VI*. It most poignantly signifies that no matter what John does he cannot eradicate from his own mind that Arthur's rights to the throne are better than his own. Not even Hubert, the companion to whom he bares his inmost thoughts however

84

briefly—"I'll tell thee what, my friend, / He is a very serpent in my way; / And wheresoe'er this foot of mine doth
tread, / He lies before me" (III.iii.60–63)—can do John the
service of eradicating Arthur's prior rights. Arthur's eyes
shall first be burned out so that John may not *see*.

Ironically it is at this point when Arthur's fortunes are
at their highest that Arthur himself of his own volition
suddenly ruins them by throwing himself and his cause
away, down from the castle walls to the destruction of
John's base courts. What avails the rightness of his cause if
he is powerless to defend it. His mother's words "Law
cannot give my child his kingdom here, / For he that holds
his kingdom holds the law" (III.i.187–88) explain the
utter frustration of Arthur's fall. John is a successful
Macbeth, holding on to his usurped kingdom, refusing to
allow his mind to give in to the "sere and yellow leaf" of
empty tomorrows, even after the death of his mother,
which temporarily stirs within him the pangs of conscience,
and successfully demoralizing his Malcolm to the point
where opposition is hopeless. All his todays are full of
sound and fury signifying much—the strong possession of
his throne.

The hopelessly weak character of Arthur conduces to the
strengthening of John's. John can set himself alone
"Against the Pope and count his friends [his] foes"
(III.i.171)—in this respect his championship of Philip the
Bastard's "I am I, howe'er I was begot" (I.i.175) is made
even further appropriate, but Arthur's cause is not self
sufficient, and cannot be by the very fact of Arthur's
childhood and his mental constitution. He resembles no one
better than Henry VI by his remark that were he out of
prison and keeping sheep he would be as merry as the day
is long, and by his subconscious wish that he had not been
born Geoffrey's son, thus inheriting a claim to the throne.

Ironically enough Arthur is granted some triumph in his death, for it is in the belief that Hubert has carried out the instructions over Arthur that John has himself crowned a second time. The nobles consider this move is "wasteful and ridiculous excess" (IV.ii.16) and quite superfluous, and John's rejoinder that he has acquainted them with some reasons and will divulge more is tempered with his remark that "more strong [then] lesser is [his] fear" (IV.ii.42). Basically John feels the need for a second coronation *after* Arthur's death because he considers his first was null and void while Arthur was alive. But now he runs the risk of his nobles' interpreting it exactly that way, and asking "If what in rest [he] ha[s] in right [he] hold[s]" (IV.ii.55). With troubles piling on this weakness, his nobles' defection, his mother's death, the prophecies, and invasion from France, a weaker mind than John's would easily have broken, but his familiar pattern of conduct stands him in good stead, and his trump card—voluntary reconciliation with Rome—sufficiently disconcerts his enemies to allow him time to regather his ailing strength.

The reconciliation is a brilliant move. It sets the word against the word. Pandulph had endowed Lewis with Arthur's rights, made him assume Arthur's claim to the throne, and now Pandulph has been bought with a spiritual philosopher's stone—"his spirit is come in, / That so stood out against the Holy Church" (V.ii.70–71). Lewis's claim is thus bought out by spiritual commodity. That which set him on now sets him off. What a deal of pains Lewis had to take to make his father King Philip foreswear his new allegiance with John over the wedding of Blanche, when the papal legate excommunicated John for refusing the appointment of Stephen Langton as archbishop of Canterbury, and threatened King Philip with the same for "his allegiance to an heretic" (III.i.175). King Philip tries equivocating in defence of his present position by disjoining his hand but not his faith (III.i.262), and Pandulph tries equivocating in defence of King Philip's former position when he was a sworn enemy to John—"thy later vows against thy first / Is in thyself rebellion to thyself" (III.i.288–89), but they are both novices of the art of equivocation of which John is a past and present master.

John's singleness of purpose is far stronger then Lewis's or Pandulph's. With him it is not a question of trying to gain something he does not have, but to hold on to what he has. This is why he is not at the mercy of the shiftiness of the presiding god, commodity. He is steadfast in strong possession provided he can bind his conscience within him that so stands out against his usurpation, and the means he takes are eminently successful.

And yet it is Pandulph's promise in the act of excommunicating John that "meritorious shall that hand be call'd / . . . That takes away by any secret course / Thy hateful life" (III.i.176,178–179) that is credited by Hubert as causing John's downfall—"poison'd by a monk" (V.vi.23) in Swinstead Abbey, whither John retreated on Hubert's news that the battle with the French was going badly. It is a brilliant dramatic stroke to suggest that John's death may have been basically caused either by the fever which he had been suffering from *before* going to Swinstead, or by the poison which he was reputed as having received there. All along opposition to John has been weak and exploited against itself, and now his last enemy, death, is denied the victory of a clear death certificate.

John's triumph, and surely there can be no doubt that in depriving Arthur, "yon green boy" of the "sun to ripe / The bloom that promiseth a mighty fruit" (II.i.472–73), and in thwarting foreign designs on his throne, and in securing the throne in his son's name, he has been successful, is obviously partly the result of post Armada nationalistic pride over foreign (in this case French and Austrian) treachery. Salisbury's and the Bastard's patriotic speeches, reaching their summary in England's defiance "Come the three corners of the world in arms / And we shall shock them!" (V.vii.116–17), go a long way to explain why in the first place Salisbury and Sir Richard do not push their own claims to the throne, and why they are content in the end to tender their love to Prince Henry for evermore. The too nationalistic vein deprives the play of possibly greater promise. It is like *Henry V* without the wonderful long first scene of the fourth Act which gives it powerful dramatic depth.

The play is entirely John's play. Those critics and actors who insist on elevating the Bastard's part independent of John distort it badly. The Bastard, in his active and chorus parts, in his claim to be seeing at one time to his own needs and at another to England's, is a deliberate dramatic projection of John himself. All the illegitimacy, zestful vigor, defiant force, patriotic fervor of John are mirrored forth in the Bastard, but they are kept necessarily subordinate to John the King, as indeed all else is in the play.

For King John as for Titus the ruling passion is an overweening lust for power, a determination to preserve his hold on the throne in spite of the fact that he knows he is a usurper and that others have a prior claim. Queen Eleanor gives him the first glimpse of himself in the mirror by her expression of the mutterings of his own conscience, but while she is alive she represents an all too convenient repository for such uncomfortable self-knowledge and her death furnishes but a brief moment of awareness to be shrugged off as quickly as possible in the pursuit of personal triumph and power. John is given yet another opportunity to face himself in all his greed at the supposed death of Arthur, but is once more saved from the need for such traumatic introspection by the news that Arthur is still alive. John is spurred on to the further strengthening of his own position by cunning manipulation of the rights of the various claimants to the throne, and everything seems to conspire in his favor. With each successive landmark of progress John has less and less need for introspection, and the blindness of John the king becomes the instrument of national triumph while John the man must live out his life without ever coming to terms with the wretched person he really is and without realizing the significance of why his feet were instinctively taking him on the road to Swinstead Abbey.

Romeo and Juliet

What tragic fools these mortals be. What tragedy of errors. They "see the ground whereon these woes do lie; / But the true ground of all these piteous woes" they "cannot without circumstance descry" (V.iii.179–81). It is not until the very end of the play that one of the participants, the Prince, sees the crack in his mirror which led to the land of the dead, and admits that because he winked at the discords between Montague and Capulet he has lost a brace of kinsmen, Mercutio and Paris, but this recognition is only a partial one, couched in terms of *personal* loss and not in terms of general responsibility, and it is too late to affect the play.

The Prince has but the barest makings of a Duke Vincentio in *Measure for Measure*. Not the least part of the tragic elements in *Romeo and Juliet* is that he did not see from the very beginning that by allowing the Montague-Capulet feud to go on building up a price would have to be paid sooner or later. The very stability of government for which he stood and in order to maintain which he put a heavy hand down on each crisis (but not sufficiently heavy to prevent the next) was completely undermined by the existence of the feud.

In some ways the Prince resembles Duke Theseus in being to a certain extent morally responsible for the feuding elements by not being objectively free enough. It is one thing to fix the death penalty on all "[r]ebellious subjects" (I.i.88) who have by their civil brawls thrice disturbed the quiet of Verona's streets, but quite another thing to help prevent another outbreak. By making immediate distinctions between Capulet and Montague—"You, Capulet shall go along with me; / And, Montague, come you this afternoon" (I.i.106–7) the Prince is showing involvement, although he cannot see it. It is surely significant that his kinsman, Count Paris, is seeking the hand of Capulet's daughter, Juliet. And this is by no means exactly balanced by the fact that another kinsman, Mercutio, is a friend to Romeo, though this friendship has tragic complications too. The crowning mistake is to commute the death sentence required by law to banishment. The Prince "rush'd aside the law" (III.iii.26) showing mercy to Romeo, who had killed Tybalt, the murderer of the Prince's kinsman, Mercutio, and in that one stroke not only banished the possibility of objectivity for the time being but passed the death sentence for the future.

The only other participant who may possibly be credited with seeing into his glass however darkly is Friar Laurence. His role combined with the Prince's would go a long way to construct a Duke Vincentio, but sketched separately it lacks obvious depth. Friar Laurence at the end of the play in an effort to clear its ambiguities "stand[s], both to impeach and purge / [Him]self condemned and [him]self excus'd" (V.iii.226–27), and sufficiently impress on his audience that nothing in this "Miscarried by [his] fault" (V.iii.267) so that the Prince is moved to exclaim "We still have known thee for a holy man" (V.iii.270) *before* the evidence of Romeo's letter to his father "doth make good the friar's words" (V.iii.286).

He successfully clears himself of suspicion of the "direful murder" (V.iii.225) in the Capulet tomb, but is by no means aware of any culpability in the initial "ground whereon these woes do lie." His very first speech in the play ironically belies his last of exculpation. Relating the medicinal and poisonous properties of plants and herbs to man's constitution he wisely states that "grace and rude will" two opposed kings "encamp them still / In man" (II.iii.28), and quickly diagnoses Romeo's distemperate condition "where the worser is predominant" (II.iii.29). As far as Friar Laurence is in a position to tell Romeo is a young man doting on the idea of being in love, loving first Rosaline and soon forsaking her for Juliet—"Young men's love then lies / Not truly in their hearts, but in their eyes" (II.iii.67–68)—within the potioning of an eye. In this respect Mercutio's teasing of Romeo about being visited by Queen Mab (I.iv.53 ff.), essentially good humored in general terms, is also keenly satirical. Romeo is a Demetrius or a Lysander in a different play, having to pay the price for his fierce vexation of a dream without an Oberon to set things right and a Bottom to project all one's silliness on as if it had never occurred.

Although Friar Laurence chides the doting waverer, knowing very well that Romeo's "love did read by rote that could not spell" (II.iii.88), by agreeing in one respect to be his assistant in the hope that "this alliance may so happy prove / To turn your households' rancour to pure love" (II.iii.91–92) he is taking upon himself the princely task of order and good government; is in point of fact assuming princely powers. He is trying to shape the course of events and actually establishing the ground "whereon these woes do lie." He does not seem to be aware of his responsibility in this general way, or of applying distemperate means to "a distempered head" (II.iii.33), except, perhaps, in his proverbial claim that "vice [sometime's] by action dignified" (II.iii.22) when it brings about "some special good"

(II.iii.18). He can wisely tell Romeo that "These violent delights have violent ends, / And in their triumph die, like fire and powder" (II.vi.9–10), and then calmly and quickly make "short work" (II.vi.35) of the wedding.

The irony piles on heavily as we are made to realise that for all his good intentions "Virtue itself turns vice, being misapplied" (II.iii.21). Marrying Romeo and Juliet is only the beginning of a fantastic series of "misapplications," the sleeping potion, the letter to Romeo, the mission to the tomb of Capulet to rescue the awakened Juliet "from her kindred's vault" (V.iii.254)—each of which increases the element of chance alarmingly. It is all very well for the Friar to say that "an unkind hour / Is guilty of this lamentable chance" (V.iii.145–46) of Romeo's death, and to exclaim to the awakened Juliet that "A greater power than we can contradict / Hath thwarted our intents" (V.iii.153–54) : what he does not seem to realise is that he set the game in motion and increased the element of chance. And there is even more to be considered than this. In allowing everything to hinge on the delivery of his letter to Romeo by Friar John at the right time he is taking more than an enormous risk. He had promised Romeo that he would find out Romeo's man Balthazar to signify from time to time "Every good hap to [him] that chances here" (III.iii.171), and yet when the most urgent of occasions arose, namely to let Romeo know of Juliet's simulated death, he sent "a friar with speed / To Mantua, with [his] letters" (IV.i.123–24) instead of Balthazar, and did not take the elementary precautions of advising Balthazar, and this when he knew what kind of a hothead he was dealing with in Romeo. When ironically Friar Laurence and Balthazar are brought forth together by the watch as "the parties of suspicion" (V.iii.222) there is no indication that the Friar recognizes how reckless he had unnecessarily been in not using Balthazar as the intermediary; he is merely concerned to exculpate himself from any of the murders in the Capulet tomb. His old feet stumble at graves as he makes his way to the Capulet tomb (V.iii.122). How many graves his stumbling will have caused by the end of the play.

Friar Laurence's attempt at exculpation presents problems too, though he is quickly absolved by the Duke's good opinion and Romeo's letter. Friar Laurence's excuse to the Prince for leaving the awakened Juliet in the tomb with her husband lying dead in her bosom "And Paris too" (V.iii.156) is that a "noise did scare [him] from the tomb" (V.iii.262): his excuse to Juliet is that the noise is of the watch coming and he "dare no longer stay" (V.iii.159), and he leaves her to what he must surely know is most likely to be the suicide from which he had earlier rescued her by planning the simulated death. Juliet's remarks at that time

> 'Twixt my extremes and me this bloody knife
> Shall play the umpire, arbitrating that
> Which the commission of thy years and art
> Could to no issue of true honour bring. (IV.i.62–65)

are much more powerfully significant now. The commission of Friar Laurence's years and art proved incapable of bringing matters to an honorable conclusion, such as would benefit Romeo and Juliet living, but again the play's irony rounds things off when Capulet takes Montague's hand and they jointly promise to turn their households' rancor to pure love by raising statues to the "Poor sacrifices of [their] enmity!" (V.iii.304).

With Romeo and Juliet there is more than a suggestion of the heady force of frantic love of a Pyramus and Thisbe, though it is obviously true that love is a triumphant force bigger than each can understand which somehow ennobles them despite their foolish recklessness. There is certainly the texture of the fierce vexation of a May dream. Romeo considers at the height of his bliss winning Juliet that "all this is but a dream, / Too flattering-sweet to be substantial" (II.ii.140–41) and in the depths of despair having killed Count Paris in Juliet's tomb half wonders whether Balthazar actually told him Paris should have married Juliet or whether he has dreamt it all (V.iii.77–79). The masqued ball at which he saw Juliet and the lightning rapidity of the courtship, marriage, and banishment all tend to emphasize this aspect, but there are important differences which go part of the way toward explaining why Shakespeare's treatment of Romeo and Juliet is truly tragically conceived. Pyramus and Thisbe are bottomed and fluted to an undiscerning audience: Romeo and Juliet are faced with their own undiscerning mirror.

Romeo's previous infatuation with Rosaline is not just a casual piece of information thrown in gratuitously nor is it, I feel, to be used merely as an indication that Romeo will be ready for true love when it comes. Benvolio and Friar Laurence as well as Romeo himself indicate that the Rosaline affair has so turned Romeo inside out that he can say "Tut, I have [left] myself; I am not here, / This is not Romeo; he's some otherwhere" (I.i.203–4). How misunderstanding Mercutio is later in his observation about Romeo—"Now art thou sociable, now art thou / Romeo, now art thou what thou art, by art as well / as by nature" (II.iv.93–95), because Romeo is apparently no longer drivelling for love of Rosaline. Mercutio had expected to see the usual Romeo "Without his roe, like a dried herring" (II.iv.39), and what irony it is that the "new form" (II.iv.35) of Romeo "cannot sit at ease on the old bench"

(II.iv.36) of love for him. Mercutio considered Romeo "already dead; / stabb'd with a white wench's black eye" (II.iv.13–14) and therefore incapable of encountering Tybalt, the epitome of "these / strange flies . . . who stand so much on the new form, that / they cannot sit at ease on the old bench" (II.iv.33–36). Romeo has merely exchanged melancholy love for the heady force of frantic love. Mercutio collapses, is shattered, without so much as a look in the glass which he is trying to hold up to Romeo.

But the seriousness of Romeo's first infatuation with love is the fact that his father and "many other friends" (I.i.152), sufficiently concerned to discover the cause of Romeo's "madness" (I.i.199)—(future shades of Hamlet)—confess themselves entirely unsuccessful. That they have not been at all perceptive in their observations is made too obviously clear by Benvolio. He, also, has seen Romeo in a "grove of sycamore" (I.i.128) and is prompted to ask Romeo as his first question whether he is "In love?" (I.i.171). The resultant witty repartee on love, its oxymoronic state, its "Mis-shapen chaos of [well-seeming] forms!" (I.i.185) reaches its conclusion in Romeo's declaration that "He that is strucken blind cannot forget / The precious treasure of his eyesight lost" (I.i.238–39), and Benvolio's asseveration that giving liberty to eyes to examine other beauties will cure love's melancholy. And the visit to the Capulet ball does exactly that—Romeo's eyes are released from bondage to Rosaline, but are enthralled anew.

The play's careful concentration on the difference between Rosaline and Juliet accentuates the frenzy of the frantic love. Romeo's regret, while still infatuated with Rosaline, that love "whose view is muffled still, / Should, without eyes, see pathways to his will!" (I.i.177–78) because Rosaline will not "bide th'encounter of assailing eyes" (I.i.219) and will not return his love, is immediately turned against him when on *mere sight* of Juliet he suggests that love's pathways hath hitherto been completely awry—"Did [his] heart love till now? Forswear it, sight! / For [he] ne'er saw true beauty till this night" (I.v.54–55). He was blindly in love with Rosaline, whom he was not allowed to see or approach in loving terms. Her decision to "live chaste" (I.i.223) and to forswear love made him a blind devotee. With Hermia Rosaline might exclaim "I frown upon him, yet he loves me still" (*Dream* I.i.194).

Romeo was more in love with Rosaline than in his new infatuation he would care to admit. As far as Friar Laurence is able to determine, Romeo's tears and groans over Rosaline were the real thing, every bit as real as his passion for Juliet. Mercutio's humorous conjuration of Romeo to appear "by Rosaline's bright eyes, / By her high forehead and her scarlet lip, / By her fine foot, straight leg, and quivering thigh, / And the demesnes that there adjacent lie" (II.i.17–20) when he has stolen over the wall into Capulet's orchard may suggest bawdily and satirically his earlier lesson that it is not Queen Mab or any outside influence which is responsible for Romeo's dreams of love, but Romeo's own addiction to love—"lovers' brains . . . dream of love" (I.iv.71). But basically it is possible because Mercutio takes Romeo's infatuation with Rosaline as real to Romeo.

The main difference, according to Romeo, is that Juliet "Doth grace for grace and love for love allow" (II.iii.86) where Rosaline kept him at a distance. But this he did not know when first he allowed his eyes to be enthralled by the sight of Juliet, except in so far as the rhetoric of her "eye discourse[d]" (II.ii.13).

The changeover is brilliantly symbolized in terms of light imagery. Rosaline is the moon—"she hath Dian's wit; / And, in strong proof of chastity well arm'd" (I.i.215–16):

"Juliet is the sun" (II.ii.3). When Romeo, making his first appearance under Juliet's window at night, asserts that "none but fools do wear" the moon's "vestal livery" which is "but sick and green" and bids the sun of Juliet arise to "kill the envious moon, / Who is already sick and pale with grief" (II.ii.4–5) he is subconsciously trying to smooth over the awkwardness of his rapid change of allegiance, but even in the terms he chooses he gives himself away. Turning night into day is tantamount to transporting himself into "a dream, / Too flattering-sweet to be substantial," but even he has to admit that Juliet is Rosaline's maid— "thou, her maid, art far more fair than she" (II.ii.6), though he tries to get round the difficulty by bidding Juliet not to be Rosaline's maid, since Rosaline is envious.

The crowning irony of this contrast in imagery occurs when Juliet, afraid lest Romeo think she is "too quickly won" (II.ii.95), her "['haviour] light" (II.ii.99), and that she is "yielding to light love" (II.ii.105), admonishes Romeo for swearing "by yonder blessed moon" (II.ii.107), and commands him not to swear by the moon, "the inconstant moon, / That monthly changes in her circled orb" (II.ii.109–10), lest his love "prove likewise variable" (II.ii.111). It is most appropriate that Juliet should think of the moon's changeableness rather than her chastity. Allowed to swear by his "gracious self, / Which is the god of [her] idolatry" (II.ii.113–14), he is less put out than Richard III, who cannot find anything to swear by that he has not wronged (*Richard III* IV.iv.372), but like Richard III "[Him]self [him]self confound[s]" by this "too rash, too unadvis'd, too sudden, / Too like the lightning" success, "which doth cease to be / Ere one can say it lightens" (II.ii.118–20).

The Rosaline-Juliet contrast sets the tone of much of the early part of the play's concern, and remains as a constant factor for criticism throughout the play. It is so easily overlooked that Rosaline is of the party of the Capulets too. She is listed by Capulet among the names of those invited to the ball as his "fair niece Rosaline" (I.ii.73), and Benvolio makes it quite certain that this is the same Rosaline whom Romeo so loves (I.ii.88). Rosaline "hath forsworn to love" (I.i.229) and is dedicated to single chastity. Juliet's disposition to be married hardly hides behind her modest claim that marriage is an honor that she dreams not of, and most significantly Juliet will "endart [her] eye" (I.iii.98) to "look to like, if looking liking move" (I.iii.97). But how willing and possibly over willing that disposition is, is revealed by several important dramatic means.

There is obviously the suggestion that her fears lest she be won too easily are based subconsciously on a lack of beseeming maidenly modesty, excuse it though she may by claiming her being overheard obviates the usual behavior. There is also the possibility that subconsciously she may be rebelling against Count Paris as a lover. The nurse's flattery of Romeo by affirming Juliet "looks as pale as any clout in the versal / world" (II.v.218–19) when Romeo is compared unfavorably with Paris, than whom she would "as lief see a toad" (II.iv.215), may have more basis to it than mere flattery. Juliet's people are pressing upon her to speak briefly whether she can return "Paris' love" (I.iii.96). Paris is also a guest at the feast and Juliet has ample opportunity to see "This precious book of love, this unbound lover" (I.iii.87) in the "margent of his eyes" (I.iii. 86). What terrible tragic irony it is that Count Paris is by no means like the ridiculous lovers, Hortensio and Gremio, whom Baptista allows to court his daughter Bianca, nor like the stupid lover Thurio, whom the Duke of Milan allows to court his daughter Silvia. He seems in every respect to be perfectly honorable and cannot help being regarded so when he goes to the trouble to visit Capulet's tomb to do his "obsequies and true love's rite" (V.iii.20) strewing Juliet's "bridal bed" with sweet flowers, and asking his killer to open the tomb and lay him with Juliet (V.iii.73). In terms of rejected love Juliet is to Paris what Rosaline is to Romeo. Paris is what Romeo might have been had he not given liberty to his eyes to wander away from Rosaline. All three, Paris, Juliet and Romeo, witness to the power of love which transcends all their limited and frustrated understanding of it.

Yet a third way of assessing the willingness of Juliet's disposition may be to weigh well the evidence provided by the nurse. Obviously the nurse is determined to assert her importance in the Capulet household on any possible occasion, and is somewhat inconstant in her championship of Romeo as Juliet's lover, but what she has to say about Juliet's weaning and early formative years may not simply be the result of her own vulgar, bawdy coarseness, but have some real basis in fact. The third scene in the play is dominated by her information about Juliet, and it follows closely on Romeo's description of Rosaline in the previous scene. Taken separately they tell us more about the Nurse and Romeo: considered in juxtaposition they reveal the great contrast between Juliet and Rosaline. Rosaline "in strong proof of chastity well arm'd, / From Love's weak childish bow . . . lives [unharm'd]" (I.i.216–17): Juliet crying bitterly for a knock she received falling on her face stopped crying and answered "Ay" when asked "Thou wilt fall backward when thou hast more wit; / Wilt thou not, Jule?" (I.iii. 42–43). The nurse gives the exact information twice, stressing Juliet's willingness. Ironically it is Juliet who now has to stint the nurse's babbling. But the nurse will never forget the incident and is concerned to remark "how a jest shall come about" (I.iii.45). The nurse's deliberate "out of breath" (II.v.30) determination to keep Juliet waiting for news about Romeo obviously serves to bolster her own importance in the affair, but much more significantly to categorize Juliet's state of mind that will not "stay a while" (II.v.29) because it is "so hot" (II.v.64).

Old Capulet's description of the "old accustom'd feast" affording "Such comfort as do lusty young men feel / When well-apparell'd April on the heel / Of limping winter treads" (I.ii.20,26–28) provided a suitable occasion for the jest to come about. Of course, he intended it as an invitation to Count Paris to include himself among such "lusty young men" seeking "such delight / Among fresh [female] buds" (I.ii.28–29) which he will "Inherit at [his] house" (I.ii.30). If Paris can woo Juliet and "get her heart" old Capulet's "will to her consent is but a part" (I.ii.16;17) and Paris will inherit all Capulet's wealth, because Juliet is the "hopeful lady of [his] earth," the earth having "swallow'd all [his] hopes but she" (I.ii.14–15). What irony it is that the invitation which Capulet sends out by a servant to the other guests is immediately delivered to Romeo as one of the "learned" (I.ii.44) able to read. Romeo, reading his "own fortune in [his] misery" (I.ii.60), which the servant suggests he has learn'd "without book" (I.ii.61), and claiming that he can read anything he sees if he knows "the letters and the language" (I.ii.63), does become the epitome of the "lusty young men" Capulet thought he was inviting, inheriting delight "Among fresh [female] buds."

The servant's remark that it is written in Capulet's invitation that "the shoemaker should / meddle with his yard and the tailor with his last, the / fisher with his pencil and the painter with his nets" (I.ii.39–41), meant only at first level to explain his own predicament in not being able to read even the names of those persons written on the list, on another level becomes an ironic comment on the whole application. Trying to match Count Paris to Juliet, as far as Juliet is concerned, is like any of the mismatchings the servant mentions. How much more powerfully significant all this becomes a little later when Capulet, exerting his authority over Tybalt storming to strike Romeo dead for being at the Capulets' solemnity, voluntarily remarks that Romeo "bears him like a portly gentleman . . . a virtuous and well-govern'd youth" (I.V.68,70) and by implication that Romeo's fair presence beseems the semblance for a feast better than Tybalt's frowns. Capulet's feast, whether he recognizes it or not, provides the hot-house conditions for his daughter's willingness, even within the very generative terms he uses.

Juliet's first meeting with Romeo belies her promise to her mother not to "endart [her] eye" deeper than her mother "gives strength to make [it] fly" (I.iii.99). When later she repents "the sin / Of disobedient opposition" (IV.ii.17–18) she is, of course, dissembling, playing for time to put the simulated death plan into action. However, there is something to be urged in the fact that she is confessing a sin which is demonstrable. Their conversation is a whole sonnet of alternate worshipping at one another's shrine from hand to lips, rounded off by an extra stanza (I.v.109–12) of comment on the "sin" which they are taking and purging. Not only does Romeo "kiss by the book" (I.v.112) as Juliet exclaims closing the meeting: she herself kisses by the far too open book of her own willingness.

Romeo's despair "O dear account! my life is my foe's debt" (I.v.120) on finding out that she is a Capulet is ironically offset by the fact that Rosaline was too. What really matters to him is not so much that Juliet is a Capulet but that she responds immediately to his protestations of worship—"Romeo is belov'd and loves again" (Prologue Act II.5). All the "blushing pilgrim" saintly shrine imagery cannot dispel the suggestion of "sin" specifically mentioned in every line of the commentary stanza. In fact it tends to emphasize the dangers of the illicit. When Juliet later dismisses the nurse because she wants to be left alone with her orisons "To move the heavens to smile upon [her] state, / Which . . . is cross and full of sin" (IV.iii.5) there is no need for such detailed excuses unless they stem from something of a troubled subconscious.

Juliet's despair—"If he be married, / My grave is like to be my wedding-bed" (I.v.136–37)—occurs *before* she knows the identity of her pilgrim who "would not dance" (I.v.134) and this cannot entirely be smoothed over by the fact that a masqued ball allows a certain amount of liberty with identities. Even after the marriage which the Friar hurries through, ostensibly because he dare not leave the couple alone "Till Holy Church incorporate two in one" (II.vi.37) Juliet's disposition is over violently hot, lacking in any marriage modesty. Desdemona's "downright violence and storm of fortunes" trumpeting to the world that she did "love the Moor to live with him" (*Othello* I.iii.250–51,249), disastrous as it is in its wedding-bed-grave consequences, is pale by comparison with Juliet's amplification on the theme—"I have bought the mansion of a love, / But not possess'd it, and, though I am sold, / Not yet enjoy'd" (III.ii.26–28).

Juliet has the perfectly understandable impatience of a child "that hath new robes / And may not wear them" (III.ii.30–31), but is whipping herself into the frenzy in which she would have the reckless runaway Phaeton whip the "fiery-footed steeds, / Towards Phoebus' lodging" (III.ii.1–2). It is by no means accidental that the dramatist has her call for "civil night" to be cloudily unmoonlit, "all in black". She is calling as it were—"[ ] sex me here, / And fill me from the crown to the toe top-full / Of direst [love]" (*Macbeth* I.v.42–44) and for thick night to *pall* her in the amorous rites of love, though there is the significant difference that she has no need of outside help except to teach her how to "Think true love acted simple modesty" (III.ii.16).

How much of her worry about Romeo's believed death is concerned with her dread of dying "maiden-widowed" (III.ii.135)? As soon as the nurse announces "he's dead, he's dead" (III.ii.37) Juliet jumps to the conclusion that Romeo hath "slain himself" (III.ii.45) for love of her and violently exclaims

> To prison, eyes, ne'er look on liberty!
> Vile earth, to earth resign; end motion here;
> And thou and Romeo press [one] heavy bier!
>
> (III.ii.58–60)

before the nurse lets her know that it is her dearest cousin Tybalt who is dead, and Romeo merely banished. In Juliet's mind the suicidal course of love's events is already evident. When Friar Laurence chides Romeo for attempting to commit suicide at the thought of what his murder of Tybalt has done to Juliet his words—"like a misbehav'd and sullen wench, / Thou [pout'st upon] thy fortune and thy love. / Take heed, take heed, for such die miserable" (III.iii.143–45)—ironically describe Romeo in terms of Juliet.

The nightingale-lark confusion of Romeo's last meeting with Juliet before banishment emphasizes that it is neither of the birds that "sings so out of tune, / Straining harsh discords and unpleasing sharps" (III.v.27–28) but themselves. Themselves themselves confound. Each may exclaim against fortune and the stars, and the introductory prologue to the play may try to condition hearers to consider them "star-cross'd lovers," but the "two hours' traffic" on the stage and "patient ears attend[ing]" should "strive to mend" what "here shall miss"—the carefully plotted course of the woefully tragic story of heady frantic love.

Juliet's "ill-divining soul" (III.v.54) sees Romeo "as one dead in the bottom of a tomb" (III.v.56) and this she attributes to *failing eyesight* when it is one of the few occasions on which subconsciously she is beginning to descry something of the "true ground of all these piteous woes." Romeo dreamt his "lady came and found [him] dead" (V.i.6) and yet tried to argue himself into the belief that his dreams of "love's shadows . . . so rich in joy" (V.i.11)—"presage[d] some joyful news at hand" (V.i.2), despite the knowledge that his thought which "did but forerun [his] need" (V.i.53) about the penurious apothecary who would be willing to sell "a caitiff wretch" poison. The time and his "savage-wild" (V.iii.37) intents put "another sin" (V.iii.62) upon his head, the slaughter of Paris in the churchyard, before as his own "desperate pilot" he rushes his "sea-sick weary bark" (V.iii.118) on the rocks of his own tempestuous fury.

Romeo and Juliet represents the tragic consequences of that enchanted blindness of *A Midsummer Night's Dream* with the fantasy world of an impossible romance and the medium of a strong potion to achieve the inevitable concatenation of events. The Prince and the Friar alone seem to dwell in the world of reality with any attendant power for seeing things as they really are, and theirs is the guilt for the tragic outcome. For Romeo, Juliet and Rosaline are seemingly as interchangeable as Julia and Silvia are for Proteus, or as Hermia and Helena for Lysander, for

105

however much Romeo may have persuaded himself otherwise it is not Juliet, whom he desires so passionately as frantic love itself with all its danger and power of intoxication. Juliet untempered by the philosophical maturity of a Julia is blinded to reality by the bewitching flattery of Romeo's attentions long before she drinks the sleeping potion. In the circumstances neither Romeo nor Juliet is really capable of seeing the essence of nobility which lurks almost accidentally in the depths of their emotions. For Romeo the death of Paris should be an awakening to the enormity of his deeds and an awareness of his true nature but like King John he is saved from the need for such introspection not by temporal success but much more effectively by death itself. Juliet alone must face the bloodstained image in the glass and find that it is utterly impossible to live with even for a moment. Her own suicide shatters for ever the dream, the magic and the glass leaving the Friar to pick up the fragments and exonerate himself as incredibly as he must.

THE EARLY HISTORIES

1 Henry VI

1 Henry VI opens with the funeral of Henry V, in which the rapacious uncles see themselves as prospective heirs. All the powers previously represented by the figure of Henry V, strong and just home government, supporter of the visible body of the church, and the thunderer abroad against England's enemies, are prismatically broken up and severally apportioned. Gloucester ostensibly represents the political body of England; Winchester the ecclesiastical; Bedford the military, and all hold power in the *name* of Henry VI, which they take in vain. The three *Henry VI* plays deal with the disintegration of these separate powers one by one.

In *1 Henry VI* England's glory abroad, ostensibly in the name of Bedford the Regent, is as sick as Bedford himself whose death "Now, quiet soul, depart when heaven please, / For I have seen our enemies' overthrow" (III.ii.110–11) is an ironical Simeon parody—*Nunc dimittis*. England's savior is not Talbot. Bedford's eyes see the shadow of the substance of England's power, again because Talbot is not the *king* himself, but only a split-off portion of him. The Duchess of Auvergne's trick to trap Talbot is crucial to the play. There is an obvious tendency to suggest that the dramatist is taking time out for an interesting interlude, and indeed Burgundy's suggestion that "wars / Will turn unto a peaceful comic sport" (II.ii.44–45) would seem to lend some support to this attitude. However, if we are not observant we miss the importance of the careful play on substance and shadow which dominates the whole of the scene and which links it with the rest of the play. What is "the Talbot" (II.ii.37,iii.16)? "Is this the scourge of France?" (II.iii.15), this Hercules shriveled to a "silly dwarf" (II.iii.22). Talbot's shadow has been thralled to the Duchess for a long time because his picture has been hanging in her gallery (just so has England's picture been hanging in the gallery of France since Henry V's death): now "the substance shall endure the like" (II.iii.38). Talbot claims she still has nothing more than "Talbot's shadow / Whereon to practise [her] severity" (II.iii.46–47), and to her assurance that by having the *man* in her house she has the substance too Talbot rejoins that he is but the shadow of himself and that his substance is not there. "[His] thoughts are whirled like a potter's wheel; / [He] know[s] not where [he is] nor what [he does]" (I.v.19–20). The riddle of "He will be here, and yet he is not here" (II.iii. 58) is solved one way by Talbot by calling in his mighty forces and claiming *they* are his "substance, sinews, arms, and strength" (II.iii.63), and the Duchess has perforce to agree "for the nonce" (II.iii.57), but the riddle "substance-shadow"—"How can these contrarieties agree" (II.iii.59) goes on. Talbot is but a shadow of Henry V and when he dies in battle, abandoned by all the other representations of the King's powers, it is dramatically and thematically fitting that his son, cast in his father's shadow, should die alongside. The death of Henry V's military power abroad is also the death of his son's, Henry VI's, power.

The force of this parallel is summed up very dramatically in *3 Henry VI* where the father unknowingly slays the son, and the son unknowingly slays the father. It is as if Henry V, in following through his father's policy to pursue war in France thereby uniting the various factions behind him and diverting attention from too close scrutiny of his title to the throne at home (and Henry V is powerfully aware of this guilt—"Not to-day, O lord, / O, not to-day, think not upon the fault / My father made in compassing the crown!" [*Henry V* IV.i.309–11]—and is painfully concerned with true genealogy [*Henry V* I.ii.96 ff.]) were unknowingly killing his son's chances to live when the battle for the *title* is joined. Moreover, in Henry VI's plucking of the red rose and appointing the white to regency of France, and in foreswearing himself over the Earl of Armagnac's daughter on persuasion by the red rose Suffolk in favor of Margaret, who turns out to be "England's bloody scourge" (*2 Henry VI* V.i.118), he is unwittingly giving the death knell to all his father stood for. Of course, father slaying son, son father, is a forceful dramatic way of showing how chaotic the state of England's affairs has become when the very lowest rungs of the hierarchical ladder are thrown so badly out of joint by the awful wrenching at the top, but the dramatist is not interested *dramatically* in the father and son symbolism merely for this exemplification of disorder. The idea of loss of identity on basic family levels need not be so forcibly presented unless there were some such bigger *dramatic* need as I have suggested, and indeed thematically it is most appropriate in the shadow-substance context.

In addition to this consideration of Talbot's shadow role there is the deliberate parallel first with Salisbury then with Joan. Salisbury the "mirror of all martial men" (I.iv. 74) is the immediate link with Henry V's military reputation because Salisbury trained Henry V "to the wars" (I.iv. 79). What irony it is that Salisbury should be blown up through the "secret grate" (I.iv.10,60) by no greater power than an unarmed boy. There are no secrets about England's lack of power abroad. What little effort it has taken to rob the oldest representative of that power of one of his eyes—

the other, Talbot, lives to avenge him, and be a "Salisbury" to the French.

And the parallel with Joan is the cruelest and perhaps the most dramatic of all. Each side claims the devil is in the other's arms; god and the saints in its own. Talbot and Joan are either fiends of hell or national saints—"God and Saint George, Talbot and England's right" (IV.ii.55); "No longer on Saint Denis will we cry, / But Joan la Pucelle shall be France's saint" (I.vi.28–29). Just as the Countess of Auvergne seeks to trap Talbot, so the Dauphin tries to trick Joan, but this great "Amazon" (I.ii.104), the strength and intelligence of the French party (like Talbot she is a strategist and knows how to turn defeat into victory, though in dealing with Talbot the operation is necessarily a see-saw one), does not mistake the shadow (Reignier) for the real substance (the Dauphin), though the irony piles on when we realize that it is *Reignier*'s substantive daughter, Margaret, who will soon represent the greatest substantive victory France has over England *within* England, the "She-wolf of France" (*3 Henry VI* I.iv.111), and that Reignier is the last of the prospective fathers Joan names for her child. Alençon exclaims that the Dauphin will be a "shadow of himself" (V.iv.133) having no greater substance than the "privilege of a private man" (V.iv.136) if the contract between Henry VI and Margaret is ratified: Reignier argues that it is the best they can hope for. And dramatically as Joan is burnt out of the scene Margaret steps in.

The parallel between Talbot and Joan is reinforced by the concentration on Talbot's being deserted by all his forces and left with only his shadowy son; their "ancient incantations [being] too weak" (V.iii.27) they are haled to a violent death.

Hellish images after the deaths of Talbot and Joan

cluster round Winchester, and the dramatist loses no time in making this transfer effective. York's curse on Joan as she is taken away by the guards—"Break thou in pieces and consume to ashes, / Thou foul accursed minister of hell!" (V.iv.92–93)—is immediately followed by the entry of Winchester, who moved with remorse at "these outrageous broils" in "the states of Christendom" (V.iv.97,96) announces the opening of peace terms with France on the basis of the Henry VI-Margaret pact.

With the death of Henry V the glass in which he recognized the guilt inherent in his own claim to the throne is already broken into three fragments of rapacity with the shadowy figurehead of Henry VI nominally holding sway over the disparate entities. Henry V had understood the need to unite church and state in order to preserve the strength of England under his own image; had understood the importance of cementing the ties at home in order to triumph over his country's enemies abroad, but even he was guilty of turning his back on the mirror by his attempt to divert attention from his faulty claim through his foreign commitments. This is the blindness that Henry VI has inherited from his father, and lacking his father's strong character he becomes a mere puppet on the stage of England's downfall. Talbot, himself an empty shadow of the military power that was Henry V, grotesquely illustrates how vain and helpless Lancastrian power has become. He is shattered in the mirror of his own son on the battlefield of his own choice which exactly parallels what Henry V has done for his own son Henry VI. Talbot is too absorbed in self-glory to see the implications of his tragic lack of substance, and his death frees Henry VI from the reins of self-knowledge at the same time as it robs England of her power abroad.

2 Henry VI

What final irony when Suffolk closes *1 Henry VI* exclaiming that he will rule Margaret, the King, and the realm, and opens *2 Henry VI* presenting Margaret to the King and referring to himself as a "great shadow" to the "substance" of the King he has been representing in the wooing (I.i.13–14).

Henry, in taking Margaret to himself, is automatically sealing Gloucester's death, the symbol of his power at home, and knows instinctively that when this has gone he will live a "double death" (III.ii.55). Gloucester, who could not command the support of the church in *1 Henry VI*, no longer has any worthwhile power—he is Protector in name only, and this is taken in vain not only by the rival factions, Margaret-Suffolk, Winchester, York, Salisbury and Warwick, but also very dramatically by the petitioners, who mistake Suffolk for the Lord Protector (I.iii.9–10,13–14). It is the petitioners, too, who introduce the Horner-Peter controversy, which leads to a duel paralleling Gloucester and Winchester, by means of which Gloucester loses the last vestige of his authority. The "weaker" Peter and Winchester ironically win by default of the others. Horner is so drunk (drunk with the cause of York his master as well as his master's wine) as to be incapable of fighting, and Gloucester is *made* mortally incapable. Gloucester had firmly maintained against all opposition that York was the best man for the French regency (I.iii.

163–64), but had to agree to let Somerset, Suffolk's candidate, be regent over the French, because the Horner case bred suspicion in York. York's rising claim, of course, spells doom for Gloucester, but it is as yet not the main ostensible opposition; it is working in the dark all the time against all opposition on its way to the throne.

The fall of Gloucester, that is, the utter decline of Henry VI's power at home, is dramatically set forth in substance v. shadow terms. In substance Gloucester stands on his virtue and innocence before God and man ironically expecting this to protect him when the Simpcox episode, which he resolves successfully, ought to have reminded him that human miracles are to be distrusted because human motives are never disinterested enough. When Simpcox's wife confesses she and her husband shammed the miracle "for pure need" (II.i.157) it is an apt criticism of the motivation behind bringing sight to the blind. Gloucester exposes the sham miracle which Henry in his blind naiveté was prepared to accept—only the truly miraculous can save Henry's position—, but the crowd refuses to accept Gloucester's exposition and terms Simpcox's ability to *run* away from a crippled position "A miracle!" (II.i.153).

Gloucester's ability to see through the Simpcoxes is ironically contrasted with his inability to see through the "pure need" his own wife suggests underlies their own crippled and blinded position if they are to "seek prevention" (II.iv. 57) of their foes and aim at "King Henry's diadem" (I.ii. 7) for themselves.

The dream of the Duchess—being crowned in Westminster—and the dream of Gloucester—having his staff of office broken in two by the Cardinal and having the heads of Somerset and Suffolk placed on the separate pieces—show that Gloucester's subconscious is working on the right lines while his wife's is not, for indeed the Cardinal is re-

sponsible for Gloucester's death—the Cardinal is haunted
by guilt for it, and Suffolk and Somerset do enjoy the split
power, the former at home the latter abroad, whereas on
the other hand the Duchess is crowned in Westminster by
Queen Margaret's giving her a box on the ear for not stoop-
ing to pick up the fan which the queen purposely dropped
for that very opening to provocation.

Even though Gloucester is innocent his giving in to his
wife by "Nay, be not angry; I am pleas'd again" (I.ii.55)
makes him guilty by omission of deed of correction if not
actually by compliance; (this is the case with Albany's
"Well, well; th'event"—*Lear* I.iv.371, and with Cleon's refusing to answer his wife's "I know you'll do as I advise"—
Pericles IV.iii.51).

In substance, then, Gloucester maintains his innocence
believing himself "loyal, true, and crimeless" (II.iv.63) and
almost in Christ-figurative terms claims that his foes are all
trying to "make away [his] guiltless life" (III.i.167) by
bringing false witnesses to condemn him. And the parallel
with Christ is further reinforced by the Cardinal, Caiaphas-
like, seeking for some quick "colour for his death" (III.i.
236) fearing the people's support for Gloucester (a threat
which later Salisbury successfully manipulates against
Suffolk [III.ii.242–43]), and by the Sanhedrin-like conspirators' decision that they have no need of witnesses since
Gloucester's life is a living blasphemy against them all—
"by nature prov'd an enemy to the flock" (III.i.258).

But in shadow Gloucester is guilty through his wife, and
what irony it is that Winchester and Suffolk have both
been paying Hume to undermine the Duchess by witchcraft
oracles about future greatness, have been liming bushes for
her. She tells Gloucester later that York and Winchester
have "lim'd bushes to betray [his] wings" (II.iv.54) and
the imagery is repeated in the Cardinal's deathbed confession when the vision of Gloucester's ghost which he imag-

ines he sees "stands upright, / Like lime-twigs set to catch [his] winged soul" (III.iii.16).

Winchester's deathbed confession and hallucinations over Gloucester's ghost (inviting parallel with Macbeth and Banquo; Brutus and Caesear) quickly and very dramatically put an end to any show of the King's ecclesiastical power. That a Cardinal of the church—the Cardinal's hat was *bought* just as the Duchess of Gloucester's downfall was bought—should call for strong poison on his death-bed and then die of a guilt complex before it can be brought is symptomatic of the lack of any real correspondence between God and God's deputy, the King. Henry comments on his own poor deputyship (III.ii.286), quotes from the Psalms, speaks Christian terms, relies like Gloucester on his innocence, but breaks the marriage contract with the Earl of Armagnac's daughter for purely sensual reasons (Suffolk knows how to appeal along these lines), stands idly by washing his hands of Gloucester's murder, and breaks his word with York over sending Somerset to the Tower. He is a traitor to his own Christian King image.

But perhaps the biggest shadow in the undermining of Gloucester through his wife is York. It is York assisted by Buckingham (a neat parallel with the situation in *Richard III*) who bursts in on the witchcraft séance and arrests the Duchess, and it is York who reads aloud the three prophecies in full exactly as they had been revealed in the séance. This would seem to me to be quite unnecessary repetition unless there were some special dramatic significance. Since the first prophecy obviously concerns the death of Gloucester, though it is worded like the Delphic oracle to sound as if Henry's death were the subject, and the second and third the deaths of Suffolk and Somerset, it can hardly be either of the latter who "framed" the prophecies. The play goes on to show how Suffolk is terrified by the Walter-water prophecy and how Suffolk fails to "shun" the castle of St.

Alban's (IV.i.33–35; V.ii.66–68). The obvious initiator is Winchester working through the two priests, Hume and Southwell. Buckingham informs Winchester that he will follow and spy on the Duchess (I.iii.151–54) but he is congratulated on his efforts by York, who remarks that it was "[a] pretty plot *well chosen to build upon!*" (I.iv.59) which is suggestive to say the least. It would be perfectly in line with the series of Yorkist underminings throughout the play—the Horner-Peter business and the Cade uprising. But whether or no York is the initiator of the three prophecies he is their *dramatic* unifier. The lieutenant in reminding Suffolk that it is under York's "hopeful colours" (IV.i.97)—"the house of York, thrust from the crown / By shameful murder of a guiltless king" (IV.i.94–95)—he is being killed in the uprising in Kent, and young Richard in killing Somerset "underneath an alehouse' paltry sign, / The Castle in Saint Alban's" (V.ii.67–68) for which his father at the opening of *3 Henry VI* says, "Richard hath best deserv'd of all my sons" (I.i.17), are fulfilling York's destiny.

In *2 Henry VI* Henry VI is gradually stripped of all the outward semblances of substantial control behind which his shadowy self ineffectually takes refuge. The virtual martyrdom of Gloucester, whose outward innocence so poignantly and dramatically disguises his very real inward guilt, robs Henry of his political power while Winchester's deathbed travesty ridicules and belies his religious pretensions and the strength of his ecclesiastical sway. Henry VI has been forced to witness the fragmentation of the barricade behind which he hid from the knowledge of his own weakness. He is left with nothing but an empty title, and tragically bereft of even a Talbot to help him distinguish between the substance that was and the awful shadow that remains.

3 Henry VI

When Talbot dies gone are Henry VI's power abroad and the magnificence of the name of Henry V's martial conquests: when Gloucester dies gone are Henry's governmental control at home and the power to take up arms against the seas of troubles which are flooding his lands: when Winchester dies gone is the religious myth of Henry's conduct. Soldier, statesman, priest—all were united in the kingship of Henry V. Henry VI is mercilessly shown as having no more than the title to all these, and the very *title* of King has no grounds of strength to stand on, and no regal seat to sit in as *3 Henry VI* opens. All that is left is a "personal" attachment as one by one it is made perfectly clear that the northern earls who are nominally supporting Henry VI are doing so *not* because his title is "right or wrong" (I.i.159) but for purely personal revenges on the murderers of their fathers—the house of York. The test of all this is Exeter, who, nominally on Henry VI's side, has to acknowledge the rightness of the claim of the house of York despite Henry's asking him whose side he is on (I.i. 147–48). It is Exeter, too, who sums up the northern earls' rejection of Henry's pact with York as a case of personal revenge (I.i.190). Henry has admitted in a most crucial aside that his "title's weak" (I.i.134), and all he can command now, through the Queen, is the various revengeful spirits against the house of York. He is a shadow of his own pretended title, preferring "[his] life before [his] honour" (I.i.246), divorcing himself from the very substance of his claim—his son, and entailing the crown to York and to his "heirs for ever" (I.i.195).

The play's concentration henceforth is on *heirs*. The immediate consequences are the murders of two of these adoptive heirs, Rutland the youngest and York the oldest, foreshadowing the murders of the disinherited heir, Prince Edward, and of Henry VI himself. The rapid see-saw of York sitting in the throne, then Henry by pact with York, then Edward, then Henry and Edward again emphasizes the temporary nature of the present holder—the real concern is how to ensure the succession, the heirs. York-Lancaster scales are kept equal in this respect—"Measure for measure must be answered" (II.vi.55). It is unfortunate for Henry VI that York has so many more sons.

The four murders of Rutland, York, Prince Edward, and King Henry VI are the pivotal points of the play and are carefully paralleled. The young Rutland wrenched by Clifford's forces from his chaplain and tutor (all ennobling aspects are done away with in the brute battle of force) is needlessly butchered; so is Prince Edward later, and both plead too eloquently for their deaths to go unrecorded. York and Henry VI are murdered after most powerful eloquence. The issue is to be fought out not in words but in deeds, not in civilizing eloquence but in bestial butchery.

Just as Henry VI is left with only a shadow of his title for whatever remains of his life so is York now put in the shade by the vigorous policies of his son Richard. York is apparently content with Henry's vow to entail the crown to him and his heirs. Edward later rebukes Queen Margaret's pride by stating that had she been meek York's title to the throne would still have slept and out of "pity of the gentle king" (II.ii.161) York would have slipped its claim until another age; but this is certainly not Richard's summation of the position.

York makes the tragic mistake of retiring to his castle in the *north,* the area of greatest dissatisfaction with the pact, thus exposing himself to obvious danger and pitting himself against quite unnecessary odds. It is as if the fire had gone out of his cause once he has had the genuineness of his title to the throne openly acknowledged by the reigning sovereign. It is at this point that the dramatic dominance of Richard over his father begins to take real shape. Richard's goading of his father to take the crown and his advice that York's "right depends not on [Henry's] life or death" (I.ii.11), since Henry had not been a "true and lawful magistrate" (I.ii.23) and therefore had no real authority to make anyone swear to conditions, spur York on—"Richard, enough; I will be King, or die" (I.ii.35). But Richard's Tamburlainish arguments about "How sweet a thing it is to wear a crown" (I.ii.29) and how he cannot rest until the white rose he wears "be dy'd / Even in the lukewarm blood of Henry's heart" (I.ii.33–34) sound a great deal more like *personal* ambition than advice to his father, though it is, perhaps, too early for even Richard to see the shadow he casts as he passes out such advice.

It is Richard who minimizes the number of troops needed to meet the Queen's attack (I.ii.67–68) and thus precipitates his father into the massed odds of his enemies, and conspicuously makes a lane to York three times crying "Courage, father! fight it out! . . . A sceptre, or an earthly sepulchre!" (I.iv.10,17). What dramatic irony it is that the dying York should prophesy that out of his ashes shall arise, Phoenix-like, a "bird that will revenge upon you all" (I.iv.36). The old Phoenix has been consumed by that which it was nourished by. York's prophecy is carefully paralleled later when Henry VI prophesies about Rich-

mond, "the heir of [Henry's] right" (IV.iv.32), that this
"pretty lad will prove our country's bliss" (IV.vi.70). Both
York and Henry realize that the Lancaster-York struggle
must now pass into the hands of the next generation; it has
gone completely beyond the bounds of proving whose *title*
to the throne is better to a question of a show of might.

The power push goes on underneath them, but they are
now cast up each on a mole hill, metaphorically king of
that alone. Queen Margaret orders Clifford and Northumberland to stand York upon a molehill, and taunts him
with having reached at mountains and only parting "but
the shadow with his hand" (I.iv.69), and they mock King
Henry's "adopted heir" (I.iv.98), the shadow king wearing
a paper crown (the paper claim and the pact), taunting
him with the napkin stained with Rutland's blood. There is
something of the *atmosphere* of Christ being scourged, ridi-
culously crowned and mocked, and this is sustained by
York's commending his soul to heaven (I.iv.168,177–78),
but, of course, York does not so much invoke the parallel
(as for instance Richard II deliberately does, and possibly
Gloucester) as have it thrust upon him. His sorrow over
his son converts Northumberland to tears but Clifford to
strike him "for [his] father's death" (I.iv.175) and Margaret to second the strike in the nominal right of "our
gentle-hearted king" (I.iv.176), but basically in revenge for
Suffolk. York's underminings had certainly led to old
Clifford's and Suffolk's death so it is grim irony that he
should be killed on a molehill cast up from his own underminings.

Henry VI asking God to "[w]ithhold revenge" (II.ii.7),
for it is not his "fault" that York was killed, claiming that
a throne "ill-got had ever bad success" (II.ii.46) and wishing that his father had left him more *virtuous* deeds behind
makes it appropriate to parallel Henry V's prayer before

122

Agincourt and to recall Bolingbroke's sin "in compassing the crown" (*Henry V* IV.i.311). Chidden from the battle by Margaret and Clifford he sits himself down on a molehill (II.v.14) and indulges in a pastoral such as his father (*Henry V* IV.i.285–301) and grandfather (*2 Henry IV* III.i.4–31) resorted to, envying that "a homely swain" will bring his "white hairs unto a quiet grave" (II.v.22,40), but Henry is not even allowed to be king of his molehill philosophy. He too is reaching at shadows. He sees played before him the "piteous spectacle" (II.v.73) of a son *"that hath killed his father"* (II.v.S.D. bet. 54–55) and father his son, and on the murderer's face is the emblem of the red rose and on the killed the emblem of the white, and the significance of the double entry of a father and a son is that the murderer's and the murdered face is both emblems at one and the same time.

Henry VI has to join the chorus of woe—"Was ever son . . . Was ever father so bemoan'd" (II.v.109–10) with "Was ever king so griev'd for subjects' woe?" (II.v.111), and immediately afterward Clifford's laying his own death at Henry's door, for if Henry had "sway'd as kings should do" (II.vi.14) he and "ten thousand in this luckless realm" (II.vi.18) would have left no mourning widows for their deaths, points the terrific irony of Henry's molehill kingship.

When the candle of Clifford is out which "gave King Henry light" (II.vi.2) while it lasted Henry is not even left with the supporting light of northern earls thirsting for personal revenge; he is for the dark. He makes an effort to embrace his adversity by claiming he is a king "in mind" with a crown called "content" (III.i.60,64), but his content is ironically mocked by "simple men" (III.i.83), the "homely swain[s]" (II.v.22) of forest keepers whose loyalty see-saws with the see-saw kings, and Henry accuses them of being commanded like feathers "always by the greater gust" (III.i.88). If he could but "Look in a glass, and call [his] image so" (*2 Henry VI* V.i.142).

One way out of his disillusionment is to commend himself to God's will—"And what He will, I humbly yield unto" (III.i.101), and when he is briefly returned to his kingship by Warwick, who taunts Edward for being England's king in mind and "but the shadow" (IV.iii.50) of the true king, Henry, he sees in Warwick the instrument of God (IV.vi.17–18) and almost in the next breath resigns his government to Warwick and to Clarence, and the two "yoke together like a double shadow / To Henry's body, and supply his place" (IV.vi.49–50). Despite his protestation that he will "lead a private life / And in devotion spend [his] latter days / To sin's rebuke and [his] Creator's praise" (IV.vi.42–44) it is revealing that he still thinks he wears the crown of content and that Warwick is his champion, "[his] Hector, and [his] Troy's true hope" (IV.viii.25). When he claims to Exeter that his own "meed hath got [him] fame" (IV.viii.38), that his "graces challenge grace" (IV.viii.48), and that his subjects, whose demands he has listened to and not delayed, whose wounds he has pitied and whose griefs he has allayed by his mildness, whose tears have been dried up by his mercy, have no reason to love Edward more than himself, then he is metaphorically falling back on his molehill kingship again.

Warwick and Clarence are the shadows of his body, Warwick because he was personally insulted by Edward, and Clarence because he had become Warwick's son-in-law: he is the shadow of his own mind. When he dies the drama of his *death* is made secondary to the drama of the prophecy that many a thousand shall rue "the hour that ever [Richard] wa[s] born" (V.vi.43) with all its gruesome

details. There is, of course, an ironic parallel with all the
thousands who rued that ever Henry VI was born.

One need only contrast the total emphasis on York at his
death to see how Henry's death is paled dramatically by
another monstrous birth of Richard. It is true that both
York and Henry are taunted by the murders of their sons,
but York's death gains from greater dramatic concentration
on Rutland and his innocence, whereas Henry's is choked
by his need to prophesy. It is grim irony that York does
not forgive his enemies—"My soul to heaven, my blood
upon your heads" (I.iv.168) whereas Henry does call out
for God's forgiveness for his sins and to pardon his murderer (V.vi.60). Not until Henry is physically destroyed,
not until all his military, political, ecclesiastical powers are
taken away, does he really begin to sway. Richard cannot
forget his words—"Indeed, 'tis true that Henry told me of"
(V.vi.69) but nevertheless determines to live with this
monstrous prophetic shadow and add to its propensities.

One further dramatic shattering of Henry VI, though he
as usual is quite unaware of it, is the parallel between himself and Edward. Just as Henry reneged on his Protector
Gloucester's arrangement of marriage for him with the Earl
of Armagnac's daughter, being sensually subdued by
Suffolk's description of Margaret, so Edward reneges on his
Protector Warwick's arrangement of marriage for him with
the Lady Bona, sister of King Lewis of France, being sensually subdued in his "wanton lust" (III.iii.210) for the
Lady Grey.

Henry's action completely undermined Gloucester, his
prop and main stay, and introduced, Sinon (III.ii.190) and
Paris fashion—"ne'er was Agamemnon's brother wrong'd /
By that false woman as this king by thee" (II.ii.148–49)
—a "She-wolf of France" (I.iv.111) into those English

125

flocks of which he would like to be shepherd, and led quite logically to his shepherd on a molehill kingship. Edward's action completely undermines Warwick, upon whose shoulder he has built his seat (II.vi.100), and has vowed never to undertake "the thing / Wherein [his] counsel and consent is wanting" (II.vi.101–2), for when Warwick fails "Must Edward fall" (II.i.191).

"Measure for measure" (II.vi.55) is indeed being answered. Henry gave up his kingdom, Antony fashion, to an "Amazonian trull" (I.iv.114): Edward in his bride has buried his brothers (IV.i.55) and has thus set an interpretation on the appearance of the three suns in the heavens at one time quite different from the one he proposed. The merging of the three suns into "but one lamp, one light, one sun" (II.i.31), which Edward tried to capture for himself by having "three fair-shining suns" (II.i.40) emblazoned on his target, is clearly to be understood in terms of Richard not Edward. Edward is first bedazzled by the triple sun (II.i.25) and then finds that he is clouded (II.iii. 7), and is oblivious of the fact that he brings his own clouding on himself. The irony of having Edward complain that when Henry "took a beggar to his bed" the sunshine of that bridal day "brew'd a shower for him, / That wash'd his father's fortunes forth of France / And heap'd sedition on his crown at home" (II.ii.154,156–58) is most acute. Edward himself is taking much more of a beggar in Lady Grey to his bed than Henry took in Margaret, is brewing thereby a terrible shower for himself from France, both from King Lewis, insulted by the rejection of his sister in such a dishonorable way, and from Warwick, enraged by the insult to his "embassade" (IV.iii.32), and is heaping the sedition of his brothers Clarence and Richard on his crown at home, the latter actually setting himself out to be "like a Sinon" to "take another Troy" (III.ii.190).

126

The "o'erhasty marriage" is temporarily mocked by Warwick's marrying his elder daughter, Anne, to Prince Edward, thus affording himself a personal right in the Lancastrian claim, and by marrying his younger daughter, Isabel, to Clarence, thus wooing Clarence away from Edward and yet securing a hold in the Yorkist camp. The first move is brilliantly checkmated by Richard by his killing of Anne's husband and his wooing and making her his own: the second is checkmated by Clarence turning again to his brother Edward's allegiance and defying his father-in-law, Warwick. When Clarence plucks the red rose from his hat and throws it defiantly in Warwick's face one half of Henry's double shadow has gone. The gesture rounds out the *drama* of the roses, the interplay of crossed thorns.

Warwick's death leaves Henry without the vestige of a shadow of political protection, and thus Henry's death at Richard's hands is dramatically prepared for. Henry's counterpart, Edward, even in his near triumph spies "a black suspicious, threat'ning cloud" (V.iii.4) that will encounter with his glorious sun. He means the Queen's powers are coming against him, but dramatic irony suggests that we think of Richard, and indeed all attention henceforth is directed toward Richard, whose Judas kiss bestowed on Edward's son sets an ironic seal on King Edward's desire to banish "sour annoy" (V.vii.45) and begin his "lasting joy" (V.vii.46) of a reign with "stately triumphs" and "mirthful comic shows" (V.vii.43).

3 Henry VI ends with the apparently triumphal surrounding of young Edward, heir to King Edward, by his father and uncles who have "watch'd the winter's night" (V.vii. 17) of the house of York's discontent and have now emerged into the glorious sun of repossession of the crown. It is King Edward's vain effort to translate the mergence of the three suns (sons, Edward, George [Clarence] and Richard) into one son, young Prince Edward. And to establish a new reign Queen Margaret is to be sent back to France; the "She-wolf" is to be banished from England's folds. But England has its own Sinon in Richard.

Henry VI must live out the rest of his life in darkness. York has already emerged as a real substantial and legal claimant to the throne. Henry's hold on the title becomes more and more tenuous, but York seemingly lacks the pertinacity to face himself in all his sovereign rectitude and tragically seeks shelter in the foolhardy rashness of his son Richard. A father kills a son and a son kills a father. Almost as surely does Henry VI die at the hands of his father who bequeathed him but the shadow of a crown, and almost as deftly is York killed by his own son Richard who sees no further than the substance of the crown. For Henry VI even his personal life conspires to undermine his already weak position while the dominant character of his wife Margaret and of his so-called supporters, Somerset, Suffolk and the Cliffords emphasizes and utilizes his insubstantial diffidence to their own ends in the overthrowing of Gloucester and through him of Henry himself. So many opportunities are vouchsafed to Henry VI to see his wraithlike image in the glass, especially as he sits on the molehill looking at the murdered father and son, but he remains oblivious to his own blindness when even his days of atonement reveal that he considers himself more sinned against than sinning. When Richard Crookback deals him the final blow his mirror already broken is irrevocably shattered and the breaker is already casting his own grotesque image in the fragments.

Richard III

Suffolk had claimed that he would rule through Margaret, whom he made Henry's queen: Richard's first move is
to rule through Lady Grey, whom he had been largely in-
strumental in allowing Edward to keep, for there is little
doubt that if Richard had followed Clarence's example in
refusing to ratify Edward's marriage, and if above all
Richard had not rescued Edward from his northern banishment, Edward would have had neither queen nor throne.
Just as Suffolk undermined Gloucester by paying Hume to
buzz dangerous conjurations in his wife's brain, so Richard
now undermines Clarence by letting him believe that the
prophecy that "by G / [Edward's] issue disinherited should
be" (I.i.56–57) is the work of Lady Grey. How cleverly 3
G's are made to dazzle Edward's eyes in the same way as
the three suns. G for George (Clarence), for Grey (Lady
Grey) and also for Gloucester (Richard) himself. The
whole manipulation resembles somewhat his father's in *2
Henry VI* with the distinction that Richard is constantly
playing with the idea of casting his shadow, is mesmerized
by the mirror effect of watching how it "Change[s] shapes
with Proteus for advantages" (*3 Henry VI* III.ii.192) con-
tinually. But Richard is not looking *into* the mirror. He
has never had any need for one, so he thinks. He was not
"made to court an amorous looking-glass" (I.i.15).

What irony it is that he should claim in his wooing of

Anne that she is the sun by which he lives, for which he killed King Henry and Prince Edward. The court looking-glass metaphorically shatters; an ordinary looking-glass is to be purchased not that he may see his person, but his shadow set against the shining sun of York. Old Queen Margaret, defying banishment, pours down her malediction on him "the troubler of the poor world's peace" (I.iii.221) and prophesies that, King for King, son for son, supporter for supporter, Queen Elizabeth's case shall exactly parallel her own. Later, Rivers, Grey and Vaughan recall her curse as coming true (III.iii.15–22), and so do Hastings (III.iv. 94–95) and Buckingham (V.i.25–27). The fulfilment of the curses recalls the dramatic pattern of *2 Henry VI*. The parallels within *Richard III* and the whole tetralogy are very carefully organized.

In Clarence's dream of the ghosts of Warwick and Prince Edward haunting him there is a forecast of Richard's troubled dream at the end of the play. Edward rejoices in making Hastings and Rivers swear their love in a "united league" (II.i.2) just as Henry had bidden Gloucester and Winchester (*1 Henry VI* III.i.112–13) swear amity and had been made joyful by the contract. "There wanteth now our brother Gloucester here / To make the blessed period of this peace" (II.i.43–44) and in all "humility" (II.i.72), casting the shadow of Clarence's death, and nipping the very peace in the bud, Richard enters.

Edward metaphorically dies at the thought that it was his order that sent Clarence to his death. It is as if Edward, conscience-stricken over Clarence, were foreshadowed by the second murderer's preoccupation with conscience, and Richard, motivated only by the reward for murdering Clarence, by the first. Richard, of course, persuaded and bullied Edward into the deed just as the first murderer of Clarence bullies the second one into complying.

130

Anne following the corpse of King Henry is paralleled by
Queen Eliazabeth, "poor shadow, painted queen; / The
presentation of but what [Margaret] was" (IV.iv.83–84),
mourning the death of King Edward—"Thus hath the
course of justice whirl'd about" (IV.iv.105). The old
Duchess of York joins her in mourning and remarks that
two mirrors (Clarence and Edward) of her son York's
princely image "Are crack'd in pieces by malignant death"
(II.ii.52) and for comfort there is only the one "false glass"
(II.ii.53) of Richard, and then the chorus of moans "Was
never widow had so dear a loss! / Were never orphans had
so dear a loss! / Was never mother had so dear a loss!"
(II.ii.77–79) echoes the mourning of the sons and fathers
and Henry VI on his molehill in *3 Henry VI*. All the sorrows of the three (two children of Clarence, and Queen
Elizabeth) are subsumed in the "threefold distress'd" (II.
ii.86) old Duchess of York. The scene is a clever parody of
the mergence of the three suns into one. The images of her
three sons, Edward, Clarence and Richard, are all merged
into the one "false glass"; the old Duchess accepts with
"shame" (II.ii.54) the mergence of all sorrows, caused by
that glass, in herself.

The death of Edward IV leaves Gloucester as Protector
of the young King Edward V inviting a direct parallel with
the Gloucester protectorship of the young King Henry VI
in *1 and 2 Henry VI,* and the ordinary citizens of II.iii are
very conscious of it—"So stood the state when Henry the
Sixth / Was crown'd . . . then the King / Had virtuous
uncles to protect his Grace. / Why, so hath this" (II.iii.16–
17,20–22). The parallel extends further in that Richard
with Buckingham, "[his] other self" (II.ii.151), just as his
father York with Buckingham, commits immediate enemies
to prison (Rivers, Grey and Vaughn) but the action is a
great deal more rapid. The rapacious uncles round King

Henry VI are telescoped into one here, Richard himself, hence the poignancy of the young King's remark "I want more uncles" (III.i.6). Richard's equivalent of Warwick the Kingmaker is Buckingham.

The series of murders is as rapid as Richard's protean reflections. Once crowned, however, he finds his kingdom "stands on brittle glass" (IV.ii.62) unless he can bring the mirror full circle and as a "jolly thriving wooer" (IV.iii.43) beat Richmond to the hand of Edward's daughter, Elizabeth, but on his way he is beset by the three "weeping queens" (IV.iv.201), his mother the Duchess of York, and Queens Margaret and Elizabeth. (A similar technique is used in *The Two Noble Kinsmen* where Theseus's wedding procession is interrupted by three weeping Queens in black).

The weeping women, chorus-like, point out the parallels. Even Anne, summoned in IV.i. to be crowned as Queen, exclaims on it as if she were going to her grave, and the Duchess and Queen Elizabeth pity her complaining.

What irony it is for Richard to be told by Queen Elizabeth that the way to woo her daughter, Elizabeth, is to present a handkerchief which "did drain / The purple sap from her sweet brother's body" (IV.iv.276–77) as "sometime Margaret / Did to thy father, steep'd in Rutland's blood" IV.iv.274–75). And what irony it is that Queen Elizabeth seems to Richard to be a "Relenting fool, and shallow changing woman!" (IV.iv.431) in suggesting he write to her very shortly from whom he shall understand the princess's mind, when Queen Margaret had instructed her "Bett'ring thy loss makes the bad causer worse; / Revolving this will teach thee how to curse" (IV.iv.122– 23). Richard's whole line of argument with Queen Elizabeth is that she better herself and her fortunes by marrying her daughter to him. Queen Elizabeth, possibly remembering Queen Margaret's advice, finds the best way to curse

Richard is to seem to give in to his persuasion and then behind his back to consent heartily that Richmond "should espouse Elizabeth her daughter" (IV.v.8).

The wooing of Princess Elizabeth through her mother presents far greater difficulties than wooing Lady Anne, and tasks Richard to the full. One by one *all* his defences are torn down, and he can only swear by himself knowing "Myself myself confound[s]" (IV.iv.399).

The series of ghostly appearances parallels the choruses of weeping women, and manages to stir some conscience in Richard—"Have mercy, Jesu!" (V.iii.178). This has been gradually led up to by the second murderer of Clarence reneging and asserting the power of conscience. It may also have been a combination of this movement and his mother's "most grievous curse" (IV.iv.187) and prayers fighting on the adverse party, whispering "the spirits of [his] enemies / And promis[ing] them success and victory" (IV.iv. 192–93). Certainly there has been some preparation for the ghastly reflections of his dreams. Conscience is the shadow that overcasts Richard and his son at Bosworth, though, of course, he would never admit it even if he were in any real way aware of it. Conscience is the basis of the "shadows" (V.iii.215) Ratcliffe tells him not to be afraid of, and Richard admits that "shadows tonight / Have struck more terror to the soul of Richard / Than can the substance of ten thousand soldiers" (V.iii.216–18) of Richmond.

The three weeping queens thus gain powerful vengeance. Queen Margaret returns to France to smile at England's woes; Queen Elizabeth defeats Richard's purpose of marrying her daughter and marries her to Richmond, the future King Henry VII; the Duchess of York's curse takes some effect.

How artificially the play is ended; the ghosts one by one

deliver their message first to Richard then to Richmond; the scene shifts rapidly from one to the other; each makes an oration, and Richard slays five shadows of Richmond before the real substance slays him, and then unites the houses of York and Lancaster thus establishing peace on an acceptable basis.

Richard is shattered. His reign was one of "brittle glass" reflecting the distorted images of his monstrous deeds.

"[Him]self [him]self confound[ed]" (IV.iv.399) without even knowing himself.

Richard III is preoccupied with his own image but the creation of his own ambitious fancy rather than the true picture in the glass. Consequently Richard is able to manipulate the reflections he chooses to see in whatever way best suits his own grotesque purposes. Murder is lightly undertaken and summarily executed in his eagerness to attain the substance of the crown and the most obviously advantageous marriage contract. The tears engendered by his deeds stir in him some latent feelings of remorse and his subconscious is disturbed by shadowy dreams and ghostly apparitions, but all to no avail. Richard's refusal to admit the need for self-knowledge results in the downfall of his ill-founded power and the destruction of his monstrous person at the hands of Richmond. It is only through the annihilation of this brittle image of power created by Richard from the shattered fragments of his opponents and through the shattering of the deliberately unseeing person he has chosen to be that peace eventually results between the houses of York and Lancaster.

Richard II

Much of the early part of *Richard II* depends on Richard's refusal to acknowledge the shadow which his would-be regal-looking substance throws. Behind the gorgeous pageantry scenes of the mutual challenge of Bolingbroke and Mowbray lurks the gruesome fact that it is Richard himself who is responsible for the murder of his uncle Gloucester, and who has involved Mowbray in the affair. Mowbray's plea that his "sovereign turn away his face / And bid his ears a little while be deaf" (I.i.111–12) is all in vain, because Richard's "eye . . . hath not heard, [and] ear . . . hath not seen" (*Dream* IV.i.215–16) the ridiculous position of trying to be an impartial judge between Bolingbroke and Mowbray. His shadow casts its metaphorical weight on Mowbray's side, pressing down his bucket of tears, so that later in the play when he identifies himself with an unseen bucket that is "down and full of tears" (IV.i.188) he is really equating himself with Mowbray, though he little knows it. Similarly when he descends to fold Bolingbroke in his arms before the intended joust and merely bids farewell to Mowbray, and again when he judges Bolingbroke more lightly than Mowbray by apportioning only a ten years' exile as opposed to a life-time one for Mowbray, and even then "[p]luck[s] four away" (I.iii.211) lightening Bolingbroke's load, he is creating the emptier bucket for Bolingbroke "ever dancing in the air" (IV.i.

186), and all he knows of this is his observation that Bolingbroke's resolution soars a high pitch (I.i.109)—"As were our England in reversion his, / And he our subjects' next degree in hope" (I.iv.35–36), as if it were totally independent of himself.

This unawareness is paralleled by Gaunt, who is but the pale shadow of his son Bolingbroke. He may exclaim that "to venge . . . Gloucester's death" (I.ii.36) is in the hands of God, and that he himself "may never lift / An angry arm against His minister" (I.ii.40–41), but he is able to salve his own conscience at the expense of his son. All his own punning on his name (II.i.72–83) is dramatically appropriate, because in accusing the King of "killing [his] name in [him]" (II.i.86) he is trying to take the gauntness out of his name, and is in point of fact drawing most obvious attention not just to what he considers to be Richard's ill and evil, but also to his own most blatant gauntness and leanness. And in making himself the prophet of England's "royal throne of kings" (II.i.40) he is indeed showing a landlord's concern for someone else's property.

What irony it is that Gaunt's prophecy that "[Richard's] rash fierce blaze of riot cannot last," for "Consuming means, soon preys upon itself" (II.i.33;39), should prove true for his son's career also. If only we could keep this carefully in mind we would not so easily fall victim to the supercharged national sentimentality of "This other Eden" (II.i.42) speech, but instead would realize that it is *the* prelude to the chaos of the Wars of the Roses. Richard's Queen in the garden scene (III.iv) causes us to "set a bank of rue, sour herb of grace" (III.iv.105) in England's garden, not just in "remembrance of a weeping queen" (III.iv. 107), but in remembrance also of a "second fall of cursed man" (III.iv.76), in a second Eden in which the serpent is

Bolingbroke. Gaunt's "This other Eden" speech seen in this light takes on its real dramatic function and ceases to be the show of mere rhetorical and sentimental splendor so superficially allotted to it.

And what bitter irony it becomes for Gaunt to wish that Richard had been deposed before he was possessed of the throne, when the whole War of the Roses conduces to wishing the very same thing of Bolingbroke. Henry VI's reminder that "things ill-got had ever bad success" (*3 Henry VI* II.ii.46) with reference to the "by-paths and indirect crook'd ways" (*2 Henry IV* IV.v.185) by which his granfather, Bolingbroke, got the crown, is the controlling factor.

Gaunt's words would not ring true as an objective choric haranguing of Richard even if he were not the father of Bolingbroke, because "the part [he] had in Woodstock's (Gloucester's) blood" (I.ii.1), his own lineage from Edward III, emboldens his bias. In a sense Gaunt is a spur to prick the sides of his son's ambition—Bolingbroke will not risk "seem[ing] crest-fallen in [his] father's sight" (I.i.188). Gaunt "plays" the impartial judge, casting his vote for his son's banishment, but hopes to reverse it as a father (I.iii. 237–38): similarly he "plays" the impartial judge when the Duchess of Gloucester tries to stir him to venge her husband, his brother's death, by casting his vote in favor of "Let Heaven revenge" (I.ii.40), but hopes to revenge it as a father, making absolutely no protestation whatsoever to the Duchess's interpretation of his instruction to her that she should rely on "God, the widow's champion and defence" (I.ii.43) as letting her "husband's wrongs" sit on "Hereford's (Bolingbroke's) spear" (I.ii.47). Gaunt and his son are reminiscent of York and his in *2 and 3 Henry VI*, save that Gaunt himself is dramatically set forth for such a

137

short time, though most conspicuously and effectively if judged fairly, and not delineated as *actively* staking out a claim to the throne.

The third son of Edward III, York, affords a similar parallel. He "plays" the part of a patient sufferer, pocketing up his "own disgrace" (II.i.168), and Pilate fashion washing himself clean of Richard's usurpation of Gaunt's plate, goods, money and lands, and tries to "remain as neuter" (II.iii.159), judging that he is incapable of doing anything else, because his "power is weak and all ill left" (II.iii. 154), where "everything is left at six and seven" (II.ii. 122). But his conscience, of which his son Aumerle is a constant, though subconscious, living reminder, shadows his substance.

From the very beginning his list of substantial "wrongs" (II.i.166)—Gloucester's death, Hereford's banishment, Gaunt's rebukes, England's private wrongs, is eked out by totally unsubstantiated ones—"the prevention of poor Bolingbroke / About his marriage" (II.i.167–68) (a theme which we would expect Bolingbroke to give at least an airing to if it were in any way either true or significant, but it is never so much as hinted at), and his "own disgrace." York casts his vote openly in support of his oath and duty to his sovereign, but, like Gaunt's his basic motives are quite different. That he should even express to Richard that his "tender patience" is being pricked "to those thoughts / Which honour and allegiance cannot think" (II. i.207–8) is a clear enough indication that he is thinking along those lines. The vehemence with which he accuses Bolingbroke of being "deceivable and false" (II.iii.84) in his duty is really, I suggest, a self accusation. The self righteousness with which he claims that the King's power "is left behind, / And in [his] loyal bosom lies his power" (II.iii.97–98) belies him, and the judgment that Bolingbroke's fault is "Even in condition of the worst degree, / In gross rebellion and detested treason" (II.iii.109) is practically a self indictment, but he is aware of none of these things.

York's show of strength is significantly in terms of brave deeds of the *past*, recalling how Bolingbroke's father and himself "Rescued the Black Prince, that young Mars of men, / From forth the ranks of many thousand French" (II.iii.101–02): for the *present* their actions are all subsumed under Bolingbroke and instead of rescuing Richard, the *son* of the Black Prince, they are submerging him under the ranks of "The nobles [that] are fled; the commons [that] are cold" (II.ii.88). When York submits to Bolingbroke and tries to comfort himself by suggesting that "Things past redress are now with [him] past care" (II.iii. 171), it is his complete breakdown. The Welsh captain in the very next scene may be excused for falling prey to ill omens and refusing to wait to support a believed "dead" King (II.iv.7,17) sooner than York for abandoning a very much alive King. Salisbury's remark to the Welsh captain that "The King reposeth all his confidence in [him]" (III. iv.6) is bitter ironic juxtaposition with York's capitulation, York in whom Richard invested all his powers while he was away in Ireland trying to capture something of his father's image which his subjects had never ceased worshiping.

Richard's later hasty calumniation of Bushy, Wiltshire and Green as three Judases misses the mark not simply because he is jumping to unfounded conclusions as he is made to realize by Scroop, for "all of them at Bristol lost their heads" (III.ii.142), but because Richard's Judas and Pilate all rolled into one is York. York does not realize this where an Enobarbus would, but his subconscious gives him no peace. It is this that makes him rush in to correct Northumberland's deafening dropping of Richard's *title* of King

(III.iii.6–8) and to defend himself against Bolingbroke's instructions to him that he should not misconstrue Northumberland's reference "further than [he] should" (III.iii. 16) by affirming that "the heavens are o'er [their] heads" (III.iii.17). It is this that makes him Judas-like salute Richard with the comment that "Yet looks he like a king!" and pity that "any harm should stain so fair a show!" (III.iii.68,71), because he himself has betrayed that kingship and stained that fair show. It is he who rushes to adopt Bolingbroke as Richard's "heir" (IV.i.109) and salute him as "Henry, fourth of that name!" (IV.i.112), and to conduct Richard to Bolingbroke's presence and suggest a plausible reason for the deposition—that "tired majesty" (IV.i.178) resign its state and crown "with willing soul" IV.i.108), so that they might suspiciously "proceed / Without suspicion" (IV.i.156–57). Too tired York relates how both Bolingbroke and Richard came into London, abruptly detailing Bolingbroke's joyful pageant and then almost emotionally breaks down in describing how Richard had no one to cry "God save him!" had no joyful tongue to welcome him home, had dust "thrown upon his sacred head" (V.ii.28,30)

> That had not God, for some strong purpose, steel'd
> The hearts of men, they must perforce have melted,
> And barbarism itself have pitied him. (V.ii.34–36)

and tries to see in all this the hand of heaven.

It is this which makes him so frantically sacrifice his only son, Aumerle, to the new "god on earth" (V.iii.136), because subconsciously he finds Aumerle's loyalty to Richard reflects on his own disloyalty, and because he realizes to what extent Aumerle is willing to do *something* to help Richard, whereas he himself against far fewer odds had simply capitulated to the ruling power push. In his pleading with Bolingbroke that his son like a "fest'red joint" (V.iii.85) should be cut off lest his own virtue be the bawd of his son's vice (V.iii.67), and in his claim that Bolingbroke kills York by letting Aumerle live (V.iii.72) he is really signing his own death warrant, for Bolingbroke's decision to pardon Aumerle amounts to just that. York's shadow has prevailed: his substance has failed. He set "the word itself against the word" (V.iii.122); tried to say "pardon" in French so that it would not be understood and valid in English. His son's support of Richard and *attempted* betrayal of Bolingbroke can be pardoned: his own betrayal of Richard and support of Bolingbroke cannot. But he refuses to look at himself fairly and squarely in the mirror of his deeds, and has set up a new image of himself which he is frantically trying to believe in.

The qualified terms in which Bolingbroke grants pardon to Aumerle—"I pardon him, as God shall pardon me" (V. iii.131)—are likewise setting the word against the word, because Bolingbroke cannot give up the things for which he bloodied his "guilty hand" (V.vi.50). He played the part of his uncle Gloucester's avenger, but in his charge against Mowbray

That he's a traitor, foul and dangerous,
To God of heaven, King Richard, and to me;
And as I truly fight, defend me Heaven. (I.iii.39–41)

he couched the very terms of his own condemnation, though unaware.

Bolingbroke, not Mowbray, will bear "along / The clogging burden of a guilty soul" (I.iii.199–200). Mowbray's end is described in most exemplary Christian terms, for he gave "his pure soul unto his captain Christ, / Under whose colours he had fought so long" (IV.i.99–100), by which time all Bolingbroke can wish his arch enemy, the ladder by which he first set up his challenge to the throne, is "Sweet Peace" (IV.i.103), something which he himself can never know. He sets the word against the word by claiming that he has returned to England in the name of Lancaster only and that he was banished in the name of Hereford. By this he openly appeals to the judgment of "an indifferent eye" (II.iii.116), but hopes to reverse the indifference in the flattery of seeing York as his father who will not "permit that [he] shall stand condemn'd / A wandering vagabond" (II.iii.119–20). And he "plays" the part of a wandering vagabond, dispossessed of his inheritance, when it helps, and hopes to revenge this ignoble state in the flattery of his friends by reiterating to them the treasury promise of his "infant fortune come[.] to years" (II.iii.66, 48) and "love and labour's recompense" (II.iii.62,49). But whatever shadowy pretense has masked his high pitch from observers up to now is foregone at the beginning of Act III when, exercising the kingly prerogative, he summarily condemns Bushy and Green to death, and tries to "proceed / Without suspicion", like Pilate washing their blood from off his hands (III.i.5–6), by listing quite unsubstantiable charges that they had sexually corrupted King Richard, caused the Queen's beauty to be stained "With tears drawn from her fair eyes by [their] foul wrongs" (III.i.15) (almost as if he were stepping out of Shakespeare's play into Marlowe's *Edward II*), and caused the misinterpretation between Richard and himself.

Not one of the charges will hold. Bushy and Green by their dignified acceptance of the "stroke of death" (III.i. 31), resignation to heaven, and charge that "heaven will . . . plague injustice with the pains of hell" (III.i.33–34) —which ironically happens in *1 and 2 Henry IV*, proclaim

142

thereby their innocence. Bagot is brought forth later by Bolingbroke to speak his mind freely against the one who wrought the murder of Gloucester "with the King" (IV.i.4) and to inculpate Aumerle, but by this time Bagot is nothing more than a spokepiece. He is neither charged nor defending a charge, but issuing Bolingbroke's charge. The whole of the Queen's conduct casts no aspersion on them whatsoever. The theme is used nowhere else in the play. It is surely meant to represent very special pleading on Bolingbroke's part. The trumped up charges cover up Bolingbroke's "vaulting ambition, which o'erleaps itself" (*Macbeth* I.vii.27). "This and much more, much more than twice all this, / Condemns [Bolingbroke] to the death" (III.i. 28–29); though this is his summation of the charges against Bushy and Green it is really an ironic self indictment.

Bolingbroke's offer of "allegiance and true faith of heart" (III.iii.37) provided that his banishment be repealed and "lands restor'd again be freely granted" (III.iii. 41) looks appealing to an impartial judge, but how cleverly he weaves a legitimate case (to have his Lancastrian rights restored) with an illegitimate one (to have his banishment repealed), and backs it all up with a threat to use the advantage of his power to bring a "crimson tempest" to "bedrench / This fresh green lap of fair King Richard's land" (III.iii.46–47). His military might marches "without the noise of threat'ning drum" (III.iii.51) all the more powerfully in perfect phalanx. His waters put out the fire of Richard's "tattered battlements" (III.iii.52). Richard's sun goes down in the flooding sea of Bolingbroke's power after one last fitful blaze. The rapidity with which Bolingbroke hastens to assure Richard that "force" (III.iii.207) will *not* have him set on towards London, and with which Northumberland hastens to correct Richard's questions—

"What says King Bolingbroke? Will his Majesty / Give
Richard leave to live till Richard die?" (III.iii.173–74),
and hastens not to agree—"You make a leg, and Bolingbroke says ay" (III.iii.175), mark the whole scene as a put
up thing.

To any potential impartial judge Bolingbroke's coming
to Richard had "no further scope / Than for his lineal roy-
alties, and to beg / Enfranchisement immediate on his
knees" (III.iii.112–14), but his threat and show of power
are for no less than all. His final ascent is not so much assured by bringing up once again the murder of his uncle
Gloucester and offering to repeal Mowbray and restore him
"again / To all his lands and signories" (IV.i.89), apparently most conveniently unaware of his death, as by York's
rushing in "[f]rom plume-pluck'd Richard" (IV.i.108) to
offer him the "high sceptre" (IV.i.109). Again the rapidity
with which Bolingbroke does *not* "ascend the regal throne"
(IV.i.113) gives the impression that bringing up the
Gloucester business was only playing for time.

From then on to the end of the play Bolingbroke is made
to sit uneasily in his new robes, first by Richard's Christ-
like trial, then by father-son difficulties, minimal in his
own case with Prince Hal, but magnified by comparison
with York and Aumerle, and lastly by the murder of Richard. It is not until this very last that there is a suspicion
Bolingbroke is aware of what he really is when he offers to
wear black for Richard's death and "make a voyage to the
Holy Land" to "wash this blood off from [his] guilty
hand" (V.vi.49,50), but there may well be here a refusal
still to look at himself squarely in his excuse that though
he did *wish* Richard dead he hates the murderer and gives
him the "guilt of conscience . . . for [his] labour" (V.vi.
41). He is projecting his guilt on Exton. "The shadow of
[his] sorrow" has indeed "destroy'd / The shadow of [his]

144

face" (IV.i.291). His remarks to Richard turn against himself. It remains for *1 and 2 Henry IV* to have Bolingbroke shatter his glass and for Henry V to accept the broken image and try to piece it together by the virtue of his own deeds.

But in Richard's shattering of the glass there is more than a suggestion that Richard is at last introspectively becoming aware of the many people he plays in one person, and none of them contented. Before he shattered the glass he was certainly not aware that in banishing Mowbray for life he was in point of fact banishing himself. The parallel is strengthened by the fact that Mowbray's death is dramatically made to coincide with Richard's death as King—Bolingbroke immediately ascends his regal throne. In seizing into his hands Hereford's properties and monies he was not aware that this was his psychological compensation for being rebuked by Gaunt and for the hatred which he complacently knows Gaunt and his son Hereford bear toward him—"As Hereford's love, so his; / As theirs, so mine" (II.i.145–46). It was a bad blunder, affording his enemy the only worthwhile ammunition he had.

In making uncle York lord governor of England—"For he is just and always lov'd [him] well "(II.i.220–21)—he was again relying on deep feelings of which he had but a slight understanding. But this time, however, he was intuitively right, for this was the very best card that he could come up with, short of facing it out in his own person, and the Irish war gave him a chance to try to prove he was "As full of valour as of royal (Edward's) blood!" (V.v.114). Richard impressed his image on York in an irradicable way, and most successfully, as far as the *drama* is concerned, shifted most of the blame on to other shoulders.

When he returns from Ireland it is only in the name of his Kingship not as Richard. Carlisle and Aumerle with him represent respectively his divine and his lineal right to the throne. The latter is to be illegally wrenched away from him by man-made schemes—"The breath of worldly men" (III.ii.56). "Not all the water in the rough rude sea" (III.ii.54) of Bolingbroke's invasion can "wash the balm off" (III.ii.55) the former. The divine shadow of his Kingship is far more powerful than his substantive self.

It is this shadow which gives power to his playing out the role of Christ first set in motion by his conjuration that "This earth shall have a feeling, and these stones / Prove armed soldiers, ere her native king / Shall falter" (III.ii. 24–26) recalling the divine assistance given to Deucalion and Pyrrha for repopulating the new world after the flood. How ironic this new world imagery becomes later in the play with the new "god on earth" (V.iii.136), Bolingbroke. From there it is an easy step to assert that "God for his Richard hath in heavenly pay / A glorious angel" (III.ii. 60–61) for every man that Bolingbroke has subverted.

Richard is confident that in the terms of his kingship with Christ he has only to ask his heavenly father and he will send "more than twelve legions of angels" (Matt.xxvi. 53), but, it must be remembered, the comparison with Christ automatically means accepting the premise that all is lost in this world. Carlisle and Aumerle are strangely unaware of this.

News of the desertion of the Welsh and of York, together with the suspected betrayal by the "Three Judases, each one thrice worse than Judas!" (III.ii.132) confirms Richard's premonitions. Even in his giving way to the temptation to "sit and wail [his] woes" (III.ii.178) there is a glimmer of greater perception that merely play-acting, attitudinizing, or enjoying yet another tear-filled role would obviously seem to suggest. Talking of telling "sad stories of the death of [depos'd (III.ii.157), and murdered

(III.ii.160)] kings" (III.iii.156), and of the antic Death "Allowing him a breath, a little scene, / To monarchize, be fear'd, and kill with looks" (III.ii.164–65) still looks like revelling in his miseries: recognizing that he lives with bread like others, feels want, tastes grief and needs friends (III.ii.175–76) suggests greater Lear-like self-awareness, but the necessary preliminary is to "Throw away respect, / Tradition, form and ceremonious duty" (III.ii.172–73) —the very signs of his kingship which he is still clinging to and which he insists on having observed when Northumberland brings him word from Bolingbroke—"how dare [their] joints forget / To pay their awful duty to [his] presence?" (III.iii.76). He is even tempted to try for a moment to angle with the "number of [Bolingbroke's] fair demands" (III.iii.123), but the overwhelming grief of the moment— "Swell'st thou, proud heart" (III.iii.140), again somewhat Lear fashion—will not be beaten down, and he rushes in to accept the fate *on his terms* which he knows will otherwise be ignominiously forced on him, which he will be made to suffer and recognize on theirs.

It is another attempt to stall full recognition of his own guilt. Indeed he plays the innocent all the more, casting himself in the role of a pilgrim with nothing more than a set of beads, a hermitage, an almsman's gown, a dish of wood, a walking staff, a pair of carved saints, and a little and obscure grave in the King's highway.

When he comes down to the "base court" (III.iii.182), the outer and lower castle-courtyard at Flint, he describes his descent where kings grow base as "like glist'ring Phaethon, / Wanting the manage of unruly jades" (III.iii.178– 79). The accent here, too, is on wronged innocence. Because the jades were unruly Phaeton met disaster. Richard is shifting the emphasis *to* the unruliness of the jades *from* Phaeton's rashness and foolhardiness in assuming the royal responsibility to dart the "searching eye of heaven . . . through every guilty hole" (III.ii.37,43). It is not until the misty mirror of tears makes Richard see himself "a traitor with the rest" (IV.i.248)—a forecast of the sending for the mirror's verification and then shattering on the full shock of recognition, "the unseen grief / That swells with silence in the tortur'd soul" (IV.i.296–97)—that the Phaeton reference assumes greater significance. Richard was guilty in his lack of horsemanship. He ought to have been able to steer a middle course between extremes, but one unruly jade in particular insisted on forcing the hand that only nominally reined (reigned) him in the direction of the rider's governing, though subconscious, weakness, the murder of Gloucester. This is the shadow over Richard in the first two Acts; this is the nominal charge to which Bolingbroke returns at the beginning of Act IV. What irony it is that Bolingbroke, who succeeds in driving Richard down down off course to his destruction, succeeds in driving himself, his own riderless horse—the "disobedient subject that against his prince is bent," with the assistance of exactly those other unruly jades that had too well learned his earlier lead down, to his own mental destruction. Bolingbroke with his sights entirely free, *insists* on making himself Phaeton—"In God's name, I'll ascend the regal throne" (IV.i.113)—knowing exactly what horses will pull him. It is Bolingbroke-Phaeton who insists on taking command from the sun god Richard. Like "glist'ring Phaeton" he is falling down into the base court of his never to be quietened conscience.

But the wronged innocence images are all eventually subsumed in Richard's playing out the role of Christ. From the three supposed Judases (Bushy, Bagot, Green III.ii. 132—brilliantly contrasted with the three *de facto* conspirators, Ross, Willoughby and Northumberland, II.i.224–300 and II.ii.122–49), to the abandonment by *all* of the disciplary twelve thousand followers (IV.i.171) and the mental flash back to his supposed earlier Palm Sunday existence of "Did they not sometime cry 'All Hail!' to me?" (IV.i.169), to the arraignment and trial with all its false and contradictory witnesses (Fitzwater, Surrey, Percy, IV.i.1–106), to the Pilate-washing condemnation to his "sour cross" (IV.i.241), and even to Carlisle's prophecy of the "field of Golgotha" (IV.i.144), one *feels* the supercharged atmosphere and tone of such a "woeful pageant" (IV.i.321). Richard's un-Christ volubility and remarkable control of the situation, for we are never in doubt that it is he who forces the Christ imagery on the present and more significantly future attention of his persecutors, emphasize the parallel all the more.

In such emotional wronged innocence imagery the well-bucket tends to weigh a king of grief (IV.i.193) and sorrows, the snow king to symbolize the melting of his kingly garments in the fire of his accuser (how cleverly the fire and rain imagery of Bolingbroke's insincerity, III.iii.55–60, is turned now to Richard's dramatic advantage), and the shattering of the glass to signify the rending of the image of the Lord's anointed temple (Matt.xxvii.51; Mark xv.38; Luke xxiii.45).

The shattering of the glass destroys the "brittle glory" (IV.i.287) of the brittle face—the brittle image of his Kingship. Like Richard III his kingdom had stood on brittle glass. Bolingbroke's taunt that Richard in destroying the shadow of his image is merely playing with his shadow is best treated, I suggest, as a revelation of the state of his own condition, for Bolingbroke's kingdom stands on a far more brittle glass.

Richard's recognition that "these external manners of laments / Are merely shadows to the unseen grief / That swells with silence in the tortur'd soul. / There lies the substance" (IV.i.295–97) indicates that at last he has begun to see the necessity of looking within at the real substance and not just at the outward show. It is as if he had awakened from "the fierce vexation of a [worldly] dream" (*Dream* IV.i.72) as he describes to his Queen the "grim Necessity" (V.i.21) of winning a "new world's crown" by their "holy lives" (V.i.24)—this is very similar to Queen Katharine's concern in *Henry VIII*.

His prophecy to Northumberland, the "ladder wherewithal / The mounting Bolingbroke ascends [his] throne" (V.i.55–56) clearly points out the substance of his environmental difficulties—envious enemies who having learnt "the way / To plant unrightful kings, wil[l] know again, / Being ne'er so little urg'd" (V.i.62–64) to repeat the pattern—, and Northumberland and Bolingbroke are haunted by this. His farewell to his Queen, which seems so artificial in its end-stopped couplets and formalized language, may be a deliberate attempt not to "make woe" too wanton (V.i.101), not to revert to such "external manners of laments" (IV.i.295). But it is nonetheless sincere with something of Ruth's earnestness in the Queen's plea "Then whither he goes, thither let me go" (V.i.85).

Richard's last scene (V.v.) certainly has the look of a reversion to his revelling in the misery of telling sad stories of the death of kings. He knows he cannot really make a literal comparison between his prison and the world, and the prison of the microcosmos of "his little world of man" (*Lear* III.i.10), but he tries to "hammer it out" (V.v.5). His brain and soul, joint begetters of profane and divine thought, know no content, because they pull different ways. Ambitious thoughts plot "[u]nlikely wonders" (V.v.19): divine thoughts "set the word itself / Against the word" (V.v.13–14), because they are intermixed with scruples about what really constitutes child-like humility of spirit (of such is the kingdom of heaven) and how far this world's material possessions (the camel) negate it. Richard knows better than to flatter himself by feeling community with all other such people who have found the world's dichotomy, feeling themselves now king of their element now beggar, but he does finally realize, even if only momentarily, that his community is with the basic nature of man, for whatever he is, as long as he is only man, he will be pleased with nothing, "till he be eas'd with being nothing."

This is the dramatic significance of the shattered glass. Man, proud man, must be shattered and made aware somehow to some extent that "Dress'd in a little brief authority, / Most ignorant of what he's most assur'd" he parades his "glassy essence," the brittle glory of his face, from a god on earth of Henry IV to the "angry ape" of an Othello, a Leontes, or even a Prospero who has to admit that "the rarer action is / In virtue than in vengeance" (*The Tempest* V.i.27–28) and has to acknowledge the Caliban "thing of darkness" (V.i.275) as his own,—"many people, / And none contented" (*Richard II* V.v.31–32) before high heaven, for man plays such fantastic tricks as "makes the angels weep" (*Measure for Measure* II.ii.117–22.)

Man breaks the time, proportion and concord of the music of his life and is thus responsible for its discords; he sets his fingers as the "dial's point" (V.v.53), and provokes the tears he tries to wipe away. He who provides the "sweet music" (V.v.42) for Richard's last stand helps him to realize what the sour substance is that Richard has made of his life's music—himself, and also reminds him to be grateful for the benevolence of the *intention*, irrespective of its result. Such should be the case with the loyalty of the groom, who with "much ado at length ha[d] gotten leave /

To look upon [his] sometimes royal master's face" (V.v. 74–75), but Richard forgets this in his railing against "roan Barbary" (V.v.78) for bearing Bolingbroke so proudly to his coronation.

This certainly looks like a return to the animistic salutation of his kingdom's earth on return from Ireland, and there is really nothing to offset this impression. It is as if Shakespeare intended Richard only to have a glimmer of his shattered self, and to have him quickly revert to his former image, because he was so used to it and uncomfortable with the shattered one. The discomfort is projected on "jauncing Bolingbroke" (V.v.94), and on the villains who rudely assault him, and Richard dies as "full of valour as of royal blood!" (V.v.114).

Richard II has the murder of his uncle Gloucester somewhere on his conscience but all too easily washes his hands of the guilt. The many parts he seeks to play in his outward show of regal splendor and kingly power allow him to forget the misdeeds of any one part in the pursuit of a title he considers his by divine right and divine assistance, however satanic the means. He sits in judgment over Bolingbroke and Mowbray without giving a thought to the anomaly of his position. Blind to everything but the outward appearances he fails to recognize his real betrayers and prefers to accept at its face value the trumped-up conspiracy presented. This ironic parallel between the apparent substance of nationalistic pride and the less obvious shadow of moral decadence manifests itself in the machinations of Gaunt and York as their sons become mere pawns to be sacrificed when necessary. For Richard the final price of blindness is death but not before he has looked into the glass and seen too clearly the fragmented person that he has become, the many shadowy parts he has ill played. This shattering of the glass seems to betoken an admission

152

of awareness but too late to allow him to salvage the pieces either of his personal life or of his public image. It remains for Bolingbroke to ascend the throne in his place and to be ever seeing in the mirror of his son Prince Hal the image of Richard that he shattered and the shadow of the guilt that he shared and will go on sharing for the rest of his days.

What Shakespeare discovered in the shattered glass technique was to afford him great dramatic richness for the future. His dramatis personae are confronted more and more with the glass of their own discontenting and discontented image. Some enter into their mirror seeking the cause and explore the "dark backward and abysm of" (*The Tempest* I.ii.50) self, the long corridor of "all our yesterdays" (*Macbeth* V.v.22) with multiple rooms of possible éclaircissement; some deliberately *refuse* to face themeslves in the mirror of their lives, knowing only too well what they will see there, and so they go on pretending; some, like Richard, have momentary glimpses that are too late either to correct a whole life's bias or to forestall the imminent consequences of it; some look and refuse to accept what they see there, hoping that if they stare long enough they will either stare the image away or transform it into what they would have it look like.

The very *thought* of the shattered glass is rich with dramatic possibilities. It is not so much holding "the mirror up to / nature" (*Hamlet* III.ii.24–25) as to the dramatis personae themselves so that they may change and develop and mirror more the audience's and the dramatist's growing knowledge of them.

John P. Cutts is professor of English at Wayne State University. He received his B.A., Honours, and M.A. from University of Reading, his B.A. from University of Cambridge, and his Ph.D. from University of Birmingham.

The manuscript was edited by Robert H. Tennenhouse. The book was designed by Sylvia Winter. The type face for the text is Old Style No. 7 and the display face is American Typefounders Garamond.
The manuscript is printed on S. D. Warren's Olde Style Antique paper and the book is bound in Holliston Sharon cloth over binders board. Manufactured in the United States of America.